D1213265

THE STORY OF MEXICO

Emiliano Zapata
and the
Mexican Revolution

THE STORY OF MEXICO

Emiliano Zapata
and the
Mexican Revolution

R. CONRAD STEIN

MORGAN REYNOLDS
PUBLISHING

Greensboro, North Carolina

The Story of Mexico: Emiliano Zapata and the Mexican Revolution
Copyright © 2012 by Morgan Reynolds Publishing

All rights reserved
This book, or parts thereof, may not be reproduced
in any form except by written consent of the publisher.
For more information write:
Morgan Reynolds Publishing, Inc.
620 South Elm Street, Suite 387
Greensboro, NC 27406 USA

Library of Congress Cataloging-in-Publication Data

Stein, R. Conrad.
 The story of Mexico. Emiliano Zapata and the Mexican Revolution / by R.
Conrad Stein.
     p. cm.
 Includes bibliographical references and index.
 ISBN 978-1-59935-163-6
1. Zapata, Emiliano, 1879-1919--Juvenile literature. 2.
Mexico--History--Revolution, 1910-1920--Juvenile literature. 3.
Revolutionaries--Mexico--Biography--Juvenile literature. 4.
Generals--Mexico--Biography--Juvenile literature. I. Title. II. Title:
Emiliano Zapata and the Mexican Revolution.
 F1234.Z37S739 2012
 972.08'1092--dc22
 [B]

                                    2010041616

Printed in the United States of America
First Edition

Book Cover and interior designed by:
Ed Morgan, navyblue design studio
Greensboro, N.C.

For my wife, Deborah, and daughter, Janna

THE STORY OF MEXICO

TABLE OF CONTENTS

Emiliano Zapata

CHAPTER 1

The Making of a Legend

One morning in the 1880s, a rich and powerful landowner entered the village of Anenecuilco in southern Mexico. Sitting on a tall horse, the man shouted out orders: all families living in a half dozen peasant houses in a corner of the village must come outside now. The families hurried to obey. In that era, impoverished farmers of rural Mexico were required to heed the commands of the wealthy as if those people were kings. In harsh tones, the man told the farm families that their huts sat on land he owned and that he needed the land to provide pasture for a herd of horses he had recently bought. Therefore, the peasants had to vacate his property immediately. He then rode off.

The people stood, stunned. Some cried. Others cursed. They had lived in those houses for years. Several families even had papers issued by the government stating that the houses and land legally belonged to them. The men and women decided to talk to Gabriel Zapata, the village leader. Certainly, he would resolve this crisis and save their homes.

Gabriel Zapata listened to the peasants' pleas but there was nothing he could do. A gloomy silence prevailed over the meeting between the villagers and Zapata, the man they so respected. Soon the land-owner returned accompanied by policemen. They tore down the flimsy houses, threw out whatever furniture they found, and built a fence protecting what would become a pasture.

Later that evening, ten-year-old Emiliano Zapata saw his father, Gabriel, weeping in front of the village church. He asked what was wrong, and his father told him about the confrontation with the land-owner and how the peasants lost their houses. Worse yet, the peasants appealed to him for help and he was unable to aid them in any way. Emiliano had always thought his father was the strongest man in the world. He was by every measure the most trusted and admired person in the village. Now his father felt helpless, and he wept.

"Why didn't you fight the landowner?" Emiliano asked. His father shook his head slowly. "The man is too strong. All those rich men are too strong, just too strong."

Years later, a songwriter immortalized this encounter through a folk song, a *corrido*, which had the young Emiliano turning to his father and saying:

**I will make them return the stolen lands
And I will quiet your pain.
This is an oath, not boasting or bluster.
I give you my word of honor.**

Is the account of Zapata and the seized land a fact or a legend? It is a story told to Mexican children, just as American children hear of George Washington and the cherry tree. Both stories undoubtedly contain more myths than facts, but both illustrate an aspect of a na-tional hero's personality. George Washington's honesty compelled him to tell the truth and confess he chopped down the cherry tree. Emil-iano Zapata's sympathies with the poor obliged him to join their cause, even at the cost of his life.

Zapata is a hero and, indeed, a legend in Mexico. He fought in the bloody Revolutionary War, which swept Mexico from 1910 to 1920.

Of all the leaders in that war, he was the only one who shunned personal gain. Zapata struggled to bring land to landless farmers. He had no desire to accumulate wealth or gain political power by taking a high office such as the nation's presidency. Always, he was true to the battle cry his soldiers shouted as they followed him into war: *Tierra y Liberdad!* (Land and Liberty!).

Pacific Ocean

Gulf of Mexico

The Mexican state of Morelos, the home of Emiliano Zapata

CHAPTER 2

Troubled Times in Mexico

Emiliano Zapata was born on August 8, 1879, to Gabriel Zapata and Cleofas Salazar. He was the ninth of ten children in the family. Life was hard in rural Mexico. The practice of medicine was primitive, and children died with cruel frequency. Only four of the ten Zapata siblings survived to adulthood.

The village of Anenecuilco, where Emiliano was born, held about ninety houses and four hundred people. The town lay in the state of Morelos, some fifty miles south of Mexico City. Zapata and his brothers and sisters were thought of as "upper peasants." They had little in terms of cash or material goods, but in contrast to their neighbors they were middle class. They lived in a two-room house made of stone and adobe brick, whereas most of the other villagers resided in huts constructed of sugarcane poles.

Anenecuilco's history dated back seven hundred years. At one time, the village was united with the great Aztec Empire centered in Mexico City. In the early 1520s, Spaniards arrived from Europe, conquered the Aztecs, and began building their own empire, which came to be called Mexico. When Spanish soldiers pushed into what is now the state of

Morelos, they were impressed by the pleasant climate and rich soil. Spaniards quickly discovered that the region was ideal for the growing of sugarcane. Sugar was a coveted commodity in Europe, and many sugar merchants became wealthy.

Almost at once, Spaniards evicted local people from land they had been farming for generations and established sugarcane plantations. Hatred erupted between the Indian people who lost their land and their new Spanish masters. In Morelos, the burning issue of landownership dated back centuries, to the time when the Spaniards first arrived.

Mexican Geography

Modern Mexico is officially called *Estados Unidos Mexicanos* (United Mexican States). Like its neighbor to the north, it is divided into states, each one with its own capital city and some degree of home rule. Today's Mexico has thirty-one states and one federal district. The federal district surrounds Mexico City, the nation's capital. Mexicans tend to draw a latitude line through Mexico City and call anything south of that line "the south" or "southern Mexico." The northern borders of Zapata's home state, Morelos, touch the borders of the federal district. Though it is really in the center of the country, Morelos is considered to be in southern Mexico.

Because of the Spanish conquest, the Mexican people became divided into three basic racial categories: the whites, the mestizos (mixed race people), and the Indians. Whites held most of the land and wealth. Mestizos were given meager privileges by the white ruling class, while Indians were treated as a defeated people with little say in the conduct of their nation's affairs. Even after Mexico gained its independence in 1821, the social divisions based largely on race remained.

Emiliano Zapata came from mostly Indian bloodlines, but he was considered to be a mestizo. To a certain degree, racial categories were as much a state of mind as they were skin color or facial features. Living in poverty was enough to classify a mestizo-appearing person an Indian rather than a mestizo. Since the Zapatas lived a step above poverty, they were classified as mestizo. One's racial designation was always important because courts often ruled against someone termed "Indian."

La Raza

Mexican census takers quit including racial categories in their reports in 1920. Today, it is impossible to know exact figures regarding racial groups, but the overwhelming majority of Mexicans are mestizos. Mestizos are often referred to simply as *La Raza* (The Race). There is even a holiday to celebrate the mestizo race. October 12, Columbus Day, is *Día de la Raza* (Day of the Race) in Mexico. On Columbus Day, schoolchildren parade through village streets carrying floats honoring the great explorer. The festive day implies that Christopher Columbus created *La Raza* due to his voyages to the New World. Interestingly, Columbus never set foot on Mexican soil. The true father of *La Raza* was Hernan Cortés, who led the Spanish conquest of Mexico in the 1520s. But Mexican historians condemn Cortés as a cruel invader, and therefore Christopher Columbus is hailed as the founder of the nation's dominant race.

In Zapata's time, Indian people were concentrated in Mexico's south. Most of Zapata's neighbors were Indians. Nahuatl, the language of the Aztecs, was freely spoken throughout the state of Morelos. Emiliano Zapata probably did not speak Nahuatl, but he was certainly familiar with the language.

Perhaps the Zapata family history dated back to pre-conquest times. One of the ancient names for Anenecuilco is Zapata. Since the start of the nineteenth century, the Zapatas held prominent positions in the region. Emiliano's maternal grandfather fought against the Spanish in the early 1800s when Mexico won its independence. The French invaded Mexico in the 1860s, and two of Emiliano's uncles served in the Mexican army, which finally drove French forces from the country.

Emiliano Zapata grew up hearing tales of how his ancestors had defended Mexico against its enemies. Other villagers heard the same stories about the honorable Zapata family. It is no wonder that the villagers turned to the Zapatas in times of despair. The family had a little more money than did their neighbors, but no one begrudged them that. The Zapatas were seen as trustworthy men and women, always willing to protect their neighbors from those wishing to do them harm.

When Emiliano was a boy, his father sent him to a church school. Public schools did not exist anywhere near the Zapata home. The Catholic church ran the only real school system in Morelos, and the church charged tuition. Though the family had little cash, the father paid for his son's schooling. Emiliano stayed in school long enough to learn basic reading and writing. He also took a course in bookkeeping. The brief spell in school made him an educated man compared to his neighbors, most of whom could not write their names on paper.

Emiliano acquired most of his knowledge through work and through stories and instructions passed down by his older relatives. When he was only eight years old, he hauled wood and tended to farm animals. His father, Gabriel, was a splendid horseman and taught Emiliano riding skills. When Emiliano fell off his horse, his father did not comfort him with kind words. Instead, he scolded the boy for being clumsy. He went deer hunting with his father and uncles and learned to fire a rifle accurately. From family members, he heard of how the Zapata men had fought with heroic President Benito Juárez in the Mexican civil wars and against invaders from France.

The people of Anenecuilco were farmers (campesinos) who toiled in fields near their homes. Their workday customarily ran from sunrise to sundown. Said one villager, "At dawn, when God awakes, off they go to the fields, and from the fields back home . . . to bed—and that is all. These men are like dead ideas."

The only relief from endless labor came about a dozen days a year when the church sponsored festivals. Fireworks ripped the air during fiestas. A band with battered instruments played in front of the church. At night everyone, including children, got drunk on the cactus beer, *pulque*. During wild drinking sprees, men sometimes fought each other and made murder the price of the fiesta. Work, mind-numbing routine, and occasional drunkenness and violence—such was campesino life in Morelos.

A man extracts pulque juice from a maguey plant to make fermented cactus beer.

By contrast, the large landowners lived as elegantly as did Old World kings and queens. Some of their houses were almost the size of castles. They were known to treat guests, at least wealthy guests, with gracious hospitality. Often the owners had homes abroad, in France or England, where they resided in luxury on income generated by their Mexican plantations. The absentee owners employed overseers to supervise their holdings. Many of the overseers came from the peasant class. Once in authority, they treated other peasants as if they were inferiors—or worse, mere beasts.

The Zapata family owned a productive farm outside the village. They grew fruits and vegetables and kept a few cows and horses. Emiliano, as he grew older, attended village fiestas and enjoyed them because they gave him an opportunity to dress up in his finest clothes. He was a bit of a dandy, loving to don the boots and jacket of the gentleman cowboy. He tended to be quiet during the celebrations. He drank *pulque*, but not as much as the other young men. When he drank too much, he simply became quieter than usual.

The young Emiliano Zapata farmed to produce his family's food and took crops to markets for sale. Despite the bleakness of village life, he appeared content as a youth. Zapata once recalled, "One of the happiest days of my life was when I made around five or six hundred pesos from a crop of watermelons I raised all on my own."

Zapata's impoverished neighbors were not so happy with their lot. Their only source of living—the soil—was being slowly and steadily taken from them.

Anenecuilco was surrounded by tiny farms called milpas. On those patches of soil, families raised corn (which they made into tortillas), beans, and a few vegetables. The milpas stood near giant plantations, haciendas, where sugarcane was cultivated. Since the 1600s, the sprawling haciendas dominated the countryside. At first, the huge farms were owned by Spaniards who were granted the land by order of the Spanish king. Even after Spanish authority ended in Mexico, hacienda owners kept their holds on the best land.

In the early 1900s, railroads came to Morelos. Hacienda owners, hacendados, now coveted additional land so they could grow more sugarcane, ship it on the railroads, and thus earn even greater fortunes. In every section of Morelos, the hacendados expanded their sugarcane fields by gobbling up the land that had been corn and vegetable patches worked by village people. Sometimes the hacendados bought land from the small farmers. But just as often they simply took the land, claiming it was legally theirs from the beginning.

Land ownership in Mexico was a complicated matter. Printed land deeds were granted by the government. Some small farmers had such deeds while others did not. Often ownership was established simply by practice. If a campesino family worked a milpa for more than a generation, it was considered theirs. To further complicate matters, a dual ownership system prevailed. Farmers owned land individually, as did the Zapata family, or they owned shares in collective farms called ejidos. The practice of collective farming dated back to times before the Spaniards arrived. The people of a village worked a collective farm, or ejido, together and divided the food and profits at harvest time.

Stalks of sugarcane

To the hacendados, eager to own more land, it did not matter if the land they coveted was in private hands or owned by an ejido. Nor were they concerned if a family held a paper deed to their property. Hacendados took land through simple bullying or through court action. In

A farmer working in a sugarcane field in Morelos, Mexico

the first method, hacendados sent armed men to the fields to evict peasant farmers. Those who objected were beaten or shot. The people being pushed off their land appealed to the courts. In Morelos, there were one hundred recognized townships, such as Zapata's township of Anenecuilco. Courts in every one of those townships were mired in lawsuits over land ownership. Judges generally sided with the rich in these disputes and ruled against the poor, especially if the poor farmers were Indians.

Lawyers for the hacendados twisted the intention of an 1857 law designed to break up the large landholdings of the Catholic Church, and they used that law to strip away the land held by the poor. At one time, the Catholic Church was the largest single landowner in

Mexico, holding vast ranches and coffee and sugar plantations. Then the 1857 constitution forbade the Church from owning anything other than the ground beneath church buildings. This constitutional measure, which was designed to help small farmers, was ironically used against them. In a cruel legalistic maneuver, lawyers for the rich equated poor farmers with the Catholic Church and persuaded judges to give milpas and ejidos land to the haciendas. The impoverished campesinos were left confused, dejected, and ultimately landless by the workings of the courts.

As a teenager, Emiliano Zapata witnessed an event that haunted him for the rest of his life. People in a neighboring village, where the Zapata family had relatives, resisted the encroachment of their land by a powerful hacendado. The hacendado sent in the rurales, the local police force. Rurales were supposed to keep roads clear of bandits, but when they acted under the instructions of a hacendado they became bandits themselves. Emiliano, his father, and his older brother went to the village to see if they could assist the small farmers. In galloped the rurales, armed with rifles and handguns. The Zapata family could only watch as the rurales burned the village to the ground. The sight of flames licking into the night air never left Emiliano's memory. Years later, friends said he would fly into a rage when he recalled the destruction of the farming village.

When Emiliano was sixteen, his father and mother died within six months of each other. By Mexican tradition his brother, Eufemio, who was five years older than Emiliano, now headed the family. Eufemio enjoyed gambling and drinking, and he paid little heed to the family's history of service to the community. Emiliano showed proper respect to his older brother when they were with others, but he remained independent from him. He regarded Eufemio as a troublemaker who alienated others for no rational reason.

The teenaged Zapata, now on his own, started various businesses. In addition to farming, he bought a team of mules and hauled goods from one village to another. In this way, he became known to the farmers and shopkeepers of his Morelos region. Village leaders knew his father, his uncles, and even his grandparents. They met the young Emiliano in his role as a mule trader and quickly determined he was much like his ancestors, a man who could be trusted.

Horses were Emiliano Zapata's passion. He bought horses and sold them, often to hacendados who appreciated fine animals and could pay top prices. Zapata loved to ride, and he gained fame as the best horseman in the state. Said one friend, "He could speed away like a flash of lightning . . . on horseback he flew." He became a trick rider in rodeos and entertained onlookers with acrobatic stunts, such as hopping off one galloping horse and onto another. Horsemanship was an admired skill in rural Mexico, and Zapata became a celebrity much like a top baseball player of today.

Zapata came to local rodeos dressed in the uniform of a charro, a dashing cowboy. Reflecting his fondness for splendid clothes, his charro outfit was decorated with silver buttons on the jacket and sequins running up the pant legs. Young women attending the rodeos and town fairs adored him. He was known from village to village as a ladies' man. His sister once remarked how "especially seductive and charming [Emiliano] was with girls."

Emiliano Zapata, right, with his brother Eufemio, left

Emiliano continued his work as a mule driver and trader of goods. Sometimes his trading missions took him to Mexico City. Though the nation's capital was only fifty miles from Zapata's village, his impoverished neighbors could not even dream of making that journey. They thought of the big city as a remote and fantastic place, as far away as the face of the moon.

As part of his work, Zapata groomed and trained horses for rich hacienda owners. He often lived on hacienda grounds as he tended to the horses. Working for wealthy patrons gave him the opportunity to observe hacienda life—the scrumptious food, the lavish parties, and the leisurely atmosphere enjoyed by the upper classes. The plantation proprietors enjoyed the benefits of education. They owned books, and they could chat and hobnob with intellectuals. Zapata developed an intense curiosity about truly educated people, the intellectuals, those who had the schooling to ponder ideas as to how Mexican society should develop. In the future he would consult with intellectuals, but he never forgot that he grew up side by side with people who could not read or write.

Had Mexico been a peaceful and just country, Emiliano Zapata probably would have remained a farmer and a trader. As a widely respected man, perhaps he would have assumed a local political office. But Mexico knew little peace and justice in Zapata's youth. Trouble brewed everywhere, especially over the dangerously passionate issue of land ownership.

A 1915 photo of a soldier in the Mexican Revolution

CHAPTER 3

The Road to Revolution

Three years before Zapata's birth, Porfirio Díaz took power in Mexico. Díaz was a celebrated war hero who served in the army that drove French forces out of Mexico after the French invasion in the 1860s. At one point, the French captured Díaz and imprisoned him in a walled compound. Somehow he found a rope, lassoed an overhead pipe, and climbed to freedom. Such exploits became known throughout the country, and Díaz was hailed as Mexico's greatest soldier.

In 1867, the French withdrew and the legitimate president, Benito Juárez, led a victory parade into Mexico City. It was expected that the war hero, General Porfirio Díaz, would sit in the same carriage with the president. But in the parade, Díaz rode far behind the leading coach. The message was clear: President Juárez did not trust General Díaz.

Benito Juárez devoted his life to the belief that Mexico should be ruled by law. Law had a purity that could uplift a struggling, war-torn nation such as Mexico. Above all, the law should be applied equally to the rich and poor and to people of all races. Juárez was born a full-blooded Zapotec Indian in the southern state of Oaxaca. He was the only Indian president ever in Mexican history. He became president in

1858 and remained president-in-exile through the years of the French intervention. Once reestablished in office, he tried to bring peace and law to his country.

Juárez died of a heart attack in 1872, and his sudden death triggered widespread disorder. A series of mutinies broke out as army strongmen and ambitious politicians tried to seize leadership. Such struggle over leadership was nothing new in Mexico. The nation had achieved its independence from Spain in 1821, but its people had no experience with home rule. An orderly change from one president to another under the rule of law always proved to be a difficult undertaking. Bloody civil wars and military uprisings often determined who would head the country.

In 1877, Porfirio Díaz proclaimed himself president. Proclaiming oneself the national leader was a common practice in unstable Mexico. Usually the man who proclaimed the office of president lasted just a few years before he too was overthrown; Díaz proved to be the exception to this pattern.

For more than thirty years, Porfirio Díaz ruled the country. Men and women Zapata's age knew no other leader. Díaz took pride in calling himself a man of the people. He was a mestizo, born under humble circumstances in southern Mexico. At one time, Zapata's father and uncle were political allies with Díaz. Though Díaz claimed to be a champion of the nation's lower classes, his policies favored the rich. The president's closest friends and colleagues were industrialists, railroad men, and large landowners. Starting in 1900, Díaz fell under the spell of a group of advisors called the *cientificos* (scientists). These were businessmen of mostly European descent who believed in social Darwinism, a philosophy that only the fittest should survive. According to *cientifico* thinking, inefficient systems and policies should simply fade away and be replaced by more progressive practices.

The *cientificos* condemned farming, as practiced in Mexico, claiming it was a glaring example of inefficiency. Large haciendas produced more crops per acre than did milpas or ejidos. Therefore, according to the rules imposed by social Darwinism, large farms were superior

Colonel Porfirio Díaz in 1861

to small ones. The *cientificos* and the Díaz administration created policies and laws that allowed the haciendas to expand and swallow up
land once owned by peasant farmers.

Almost nine out of every ten Mexicans lived in farming communities during the Díaz years. Land ownership changed radically under his
rule. Records show that in 1895, 20 percent of the population owned
either a small plot of land or a share in an ejido; in 1910, only 2 percent were landowners. In sharp contrast, the rich grew richer. During
the Díaz years, a few hundred families acquired one-fifth of Mexico's
total landmass. One fabulously rich family owned some fifty ranches,
totaling 7 million acres.

Water, a precious resource, also fell under hacienda control. The mountains of central and southern Mexico are blessed with ample sunlight and generally rich soil. The city of Cuernavaca, the capital of Zapata's state of Morelos, is called the "land of eternal spring" because it is never too hot or overly cold. But rainfall is a flaw in this almost ideal climate picture. Rain is seasonal in the Mexican mountains. The rainy season extends from June through early October. If rain fails to fall during those few months, crops will whither and die. It is no wonder that in ancient times the rain god was the most important deity in the people's pantheon. Hacienda owners had the funds to divert streams onto their land and to tap into underground water sources. Small farmers lacked any form of irrigation and were completely dependent on the fickle seasonal rains.

With Díaz in command, Mexico made great strides in its march to become an industrial state. Crews laid down more than 9,000 miles of railroad track during his time in office. Factories developed, especially in the north, and the production of manufactured goods more than doubled. Agricultural output also surged as huge plantations and haciendas raised sugar, coffee, and cotton. But these statistics masked a cruel side of Mexican life. Díaz was a dictator who smashed those who dared to oppose him. He ignored social welfare programs. Mexico channeled money to maintain its army, but it spent little on public schools. In 1910, only about 15 percent of the population could read or write.

Sugar remained gold in Zapata's state of Morelos, which was called "Mexico's sugar bowl." In 1908, twenty-four Morelos haciendas produced more than one-third of the nation's sugar. Overall, Mexico was the third largest sugar exporter in the world. This generous harvest came at the expense of the small farmer, whose land was absorbed by the ever-expanding sugar plantations. Many Morelos farmers, deprived of their best land, abandoned their fields and went to work as

Smoke from a burning sugarcane field in Colima, Mexico

hired hands for the haciendas. Whole villages disappeared. Zapata's own township of Anenecuilco was reduced from 411 residents in 1900 to 371 in 1910.

Once they lost their land, the campesinos of Morelos had no choice but to seek employment. They gravitated to the haciendas because hacienda owners were the only ones in the state willing to hire people. As dependence on their bosses grew, the workers and their families moved into hacienda housing, where they became little more than slaves. Workers were subject to the whims of the plantation overseer, and many of those men were brutes. Hacienda field hands who spoke against their bosses could be tied to a whipping post and lashed.

No laws protected the rights of Mexican laborers. Hacienda workers worshiped at the hacienda church. When sick, they were treated by the hacienda doctor, if the hacienda employed one. Their average wage totaled 35 *centavos* a day, which was similar to the farm pay scale of a hundred years earlier. Meanwhile, the price of tortillas and beans, practically the only food a peon could afford, more than doubled. A family headed by a hacienda worker fell into debt to the hated company-owned store, the *tienda de raya*. Company-owned stores always charged more for goods than did independent stores, but they granted credit. Haciendas subtracted debts from a worker's already meager wages, and on payday a family saw no cash. Instead, the family received a statement saying how much it still owed the company store.

Always, the big plantations expanded at the expense of the campesino. Backed by the courts, thirty-six haciendas came to own 25 percent of the land in Morelos. Almost all the state's fertile and well-watered land fell into hacendado hands. Small farmers continued to appeal to the court system as their only protection.

In 1909, some eighty peasant farmers in Anenecuilco signed a petition (most of them simply put an X on the paper because they were unable to write) to form a legal group to represent them in land disputes. Appearing on that petition was the name Emiliano Zapata. Shortly after they signed the paper, many men in the group were arrested on trumped-up charges. Others were mysteriously beaten up by strangers. Thirty-year-old Emiliano Zapata received a notice to serve in the Mexican army. Being drafted into the army was a common punishment for Mexican men deemed by authorities to be "troublemakers."

Zapata's stay in the army lasted only a few months. He was rescued by a wealthy hacienda owner named Ignacio de la Torre y Mier, who happened to be Porfirio Díaz's son-in-law. Torre y Mier knew of Zapata's extraordinary skills with horses and employed him to work as a groom on his sprawling ranch near Mexico City. With the hacienda owner's political influence, Zapata was excused from the army. Zapata appreciated this intervention and was happy to work for Torre y Mier. But Zapata was at a stage of life where his social awareness and critical views of his society were growing. While living on the wealthy ranch, he noted something that made him bitter: The horses' stalls were made of marble and were far superior to the dirt-floored huts that housed Morelos peasants.

By the summer of 1910, Zapata returned to the village of Anencuilco. His elderly uncle had recently stepped down from his position as village chief, and the townspeople asked Emiliano to take his uncle's place. He agreed, and he was given documents that the elders of the community told him were precious. The documents included written deeds, some dating back to the 1600s, that proved that the villagers had legal claim to land that recently had been taken from them and was now held by the haciendas.

Court records within the reams of documents recounted the futile attempts made by the local people to regain their landholdings through legal means. Zapata kept the documents in a tin box. In the years that followed, when he pondered halting revolutionary warfare and turning to the courts for justice, he opened that tin box. He then studied record after record that told of the dismal experiences the farmers had with the justice system. Each time he looked into the tin box, it reaffirmed his belief that only war would return the land to the people.

As Zapata accepted the position of village leader, his nation slipped closer to revolution. The armed upheaval began far to the north with the idealism of a wealthy ranch owner. Francisco Madero boldly challenged Porfirio Díaz's absolute leadership of Mexico. Madero was a rich landowner from the state of Coahuila. Although he was one of the wealthiest men in the country, he was known to feed the children of his ranch hands in his own dining room. Thin, balding, and only a little more than five feet tall, Madero did not look like an imposing politician. Even his personal habits seemed out of place in the manly world of Mexican politics. Madero did not drink alcohol or smoke tobacco. He believed in a mystical form of religion, and in times of deep sorrow he claimed he could speak with the spirit of his long-dead brother.

In 1908, Madero made the shocking announcement that he was running for president. For more than thirty years, no one dreamed of

A nineteenth-century painting of women working on a hacienda in Mexico

vying for high office and upsetting President Díaz. Elections in Mexico were rigged, and serious opponents who dared to criticize the president were imprisoned. At first, Díaz refused to take Madero seriously, sometimes calling him "that little bird." But as he traveled the country making speeches, the politician from the north drew greater and greater crowds. Díaz reacted predictably: he had Madero thrown in jail.

Madero was imprisoned for a brief period in the northern town of San Louis Potosí. His time in jail altered his thinking. He hated violence, but he began to believe that only armed rebellion could unseat Díaz and his government. From his jail cell, Madero wrote the Plan of San Louis Potosí, a document urging Mexicans to gather rifles and overthrow their president. The Plan of San Louis Potosí was the first of several "Plans" Mexicans would fight and die for over the next ten years.

In Morelos, Zapata was aware of Madero and his Plan of San Louis Potosí. For many months, he had pondered similar actions. Already Zapata, and other peasant leaders in the south, had discussed taking up arms to defend their tiny landholdings from the haciendas. One long-standing dispute was with a hacienda with the unusual name of Hospital (there was no actual hospital there). Peasants asked Hospital Hacienda if they could rent a small lot in order to grow the corn and beans needed to feed their families. Just a few years earlier, Hospital had seized that same lot from the villagers. The Hospital manager, who regarded the townspeople as troublesome malcontents, fired off a note: "If that bunch from Anenecuilco wants to farm, let them farm in a flowerpot, because they're not getting any land [from me]"

Zapata and the villagers saw no choice other than warfare with the haciendas. If they did not fight for land, they would have to watch their families starve.

While Zapata and much of southern Mexico prepared for war, two men met in the north. The two would lead Mexico into revolution, but they could not be more different from each other. One was the idealistic politician, Francisco Madero; the other was a bandit named Francisco "Pancho" Villa.

"God brought me into the world to battle," Pancho Villa once remarked. Villa admitted to being a highway robber, a bank robber, and a cattle rustler. He claimed fate forced him into the life of an outlaw. Villa was born to an impoverished farm family in the northern state of Durango. When he was a teenager, according to a story Villa often told, a rich landowner raped his sister. He shot the man dead, and then he joined a bandit gang to escape the law. Soon Villa headed that gang and became the most feared bandido in northern Mexico.

In 1910, a strange alliance formed between Villa, a warrior, and Madero, a man who abhorred violence. Madero convinced Villa to be his general and lead the revolutionary armies. He prayed that the warfare stage of the revolution would be short and relatively bloodless.

Pancho Villa gathered an army in northern Mexico. Many of his soldiers were landless farmers or out-of-work ranch hands, but many were also bandits wanted by the law. Villa's army raided huge ranches, rustled cattle, sold the cattle, and used the money to buy rifles from dealers in the United States. Ostensibly, Villa served under the guidance of Franscico Madero, the man he thought would soon become the legitimate president of Mexico. From the beginning, however, Villa's brand of revolutionary fighting had an "us verses them" theme. Pancho Villa's war pitted the poor against the rich and fostered class hatred.

In Zapata country to the south, the issues were more basic and more immediate. The small farmers of Morelos looked to the sky and wondered how they would feed their families. In May of 1910, they saw clouds gather above the mountains every afternoon and knew the rainy season would soon begin. They had to plant their corn and beans soon or else their families would face severe hunger. However, they had no land because courts awarded their milpas to their powerful neighbors. Again they appealed to the Hospital Hacienda, once more asking simply to rent some of its excess fields. In a letter, the farmers pleaded, "As the rainy season is about to begin, we poor working men must be getting the land ready for planting. . . ." Once more, Hospital turned down the request. This time, in order to spite the villagers of Anencuilco, the Hospital manager rented land to peasant farmers from the nearby township of Villa de Ayala.

Emiliano Zapata had been in Mexico City as the rainy season approached. When he returned to Anencuilco in the summer of 1910, he saw a village in despair. The rains had started and the townspeople were without land to plant crops. Zapata called a village-wide meeting. It was a noisy gathering as men cursed the actions of Hospital Hacienda. Zapata called for order, and the meeting grew silent. He chose eighty of the strongest young men and formed them into what he loosely named an army. The men searched the village for whatever weapons they could gather. Some found a few ancient rifles, but most came up only with the long knives—machetes—used by farmers to cut crops.

So armed, Zapata and his followers marched to the disputed field. There they saw farmers from the Villa de Ayala working the land. Zapata told the farmers he had no quarrel with them, but they farmed on land that rightfully belonged to the people of Anencuilco. The Villa de Ayala farmers put down their tools and left. With them retreated the few field guards employed by the Hospital Hacienda.

Once in possession of the land, Zapata ordered the men with the best weapons to form a defensive line protecting the precious field. He then allotted the land to different farmers, giving preference to those whose families owned the fields before the government allowed Hospital to expand. In this manner, the soldier/farmers tilled the soil. This usurpation of Hospital's field was the first aggressive action taken by Emiliano Zapata in southern Mexico. Many more Zapata-led efforts would take place during the Mexican Revolution of 1910-20.

Emiliano Zapata, as depicted on a wall painting in Mexico

CHAPTER 4

A Revolution Begins

In the spring of 1910, an Englishwoman named Rosa King moved to Cuernavaca. She came from a well-to-do family that had lost most of its money due to some unsound investments. Now in Mexico, she hoped to build a new life for her and her daughter as the manager and owner of a small hotel, the Bella Vista, which catered to wealthy guests. She did not know she was about to be a close-up witness to a revolution in southern Mexico led by a man named Emiliano Zapata.

In King's book *Tempest Over Mexico*, published in 1935, she noted the attitudes of the rich hacendados who came to her tearoom to enjoy English tea and cakes. Most of the hacienda owners lived in Mexico City or in European capitals and visited their holdings only once or twice a year. "[The] hacendados of Morelos were notoriously never at home," she wrote. "And a bad thing that was for them at the end. . . . They thought of the land in terms of the golden stream that flowed from it into their laps. If they lived more at home on their haciendas they would have seen that the golden stream was tainted with the sweat and blood of their laborers."

King's sympathies lay with the poor, but she kept her inclinations secret because she did not want to alienate her wealthy hotel guests.

Only in her book, published years after the Revolution, did she reveal her hidden feelings. Especially, she felt pity toward the hacienda workers. "Overseers would drive the peons, with whips if necessary," she wrote. "I would see the poor wretches [the workers], their feet always bare and hardened like stones, their backs bent under burdens too heavy for a horse or a mule, treated as people with hearts would not treat animals. They could not leave, because they were bound to the land like serfs, by their debt to the hacienda store."

As an outsider, King heard arguments from both sides. The rich complained about the peasants—their drunkenness and what they called their laziness and their sloppy habits. The upper classes concluded that the poor people of Morelos "lived like beasts because they had no capacity for anything better." From the peasants, she heard and saw despair. Steadily they were pushed off the land that their families had farmed for generations and forced to work for the hacendados on their terms. Also, she heard the name of a mystery man. One of her land-owning guests said, "There's a fellow . . . —Emiliano Zapata's his name—who's been stirring up the people."

Zapata was fortunate in that he too had a foot in two worlds. He was a well-dressed horse trader who the locals admired, and he had a history of working as a dirt farmer just like them. Moreover, he was strong and decisive, "a man with pants on," as the expression went, meaning he stood out among other men. Also, he was assuming leadership over a people willing to fight an enemy that had oppressed them for generations. The people cried out for a brave leader, one who cast dangers aside. In the years to come, no one would question Emiliano Zapata's raw courage.

One day, Zapata spoke before a group of campesinos in the plaza of the town of Jojutla. He did not know that government-paid snipers lurked in the town's major buildings. An observer said: "He was in the middle of the plaza on horseback . . . when suddenly a shot sounded. At first no one realized what had happened . . . but Zapata felt his hat tilt; he took it off and saw there was a hole in it. . . . [He] looked toward the town hall and saw the man who had fired rushing away from one of the balconies. . . . Those nearest Zapata were about to charge when Zapata shouted, 'No one move!'"

Zapata drove his horse into the government building, galloped up steps, and, still mounted, went from room to upstairs room. He never found the sniper, and after a few minutes he gave up the quest. The observer continued, "[He had] the horse descend the steps and [he] reappeared on the plaza, perfectly calm, to the admiration of his troops and the large crowd watching."

Many campesino meetings were held in Morelos and the rest of the south. Hatred of the upper classes boiled over when small farmers gathered to discuss their grievances. Racial hatred was always present as an old cry to war sounded out: "Death to the *gachupines!*" A hundred years earlier, those words drove Mexicans to fight their Spanish overlords. *Gachupines* were members of the Spanish upper class, the despised whites who once ruled much of Mexico. Southern Mexico was home to most of the country's Indians. Now, generations after the War of Independence, the landless Indians were still being ruled by whites, as most of the hacendados were of European descent. Whereas the rebellion in northern Mexico was largely a contest of rich versus poor, the revolution in the south loomed as a race war.

Despite widespread discontent, the nation was caught up in a festive mood. In September 1910, all attention focused on Mexico City and the great celebration planned there. It was the *Centenario*, the one hundredth anniversary of the Mexican War of Independence, which had freed the country from Spain. On September 16, 1810, Father Miguel Hidalgo y Castillo, a parish priest from the town of Dolores, had given a fiery speech to a gathering of farmers. No one knows exactly what Father Hidalgo said, but the address became immortalized as the *Grito de Hidalgo* (Cry of Hidalgo). The *Grito* was one of the great moments in Mexican history because Hidalgo's words filled the masses with strength and sent them marching off to fight a vastly superior Spanish army. Patriotic Mexicans now flocked to their capital to honor the hundredth anniversary of the famous *Grito*.

Mexican independence leader Miguel Hidalgo delivering the *Grito de Dolores*. The painting is on display in the house where Hidalgo lived from 1804 to 1810 in the town of Dolores Hidalgo, in Guanajuato state, Mexico.

Mexican Independence Day

To this day, Mexican independence is one of the most festive holidays celebrated within the country and by Mexicans living abroad. In Mexico, people gather at town squares on the night of September 15 to hear the *Grito de Hidalgo*, or as it is sometimes called the *Grito de Dolores*. The *Grito* is a patriotic speech usually given by the mayor of the town. While shouting out *"Viva la Independencia!"* and *"Viva Mexico!"* the speaker tells the audience of the sacrifices made by the heroes of the independence movement. The next day, September 16, is the official Mexican Independence Day; it is memorialized with parades and band music.

The hotel owner, Rosa King, journeyed north to Mexico City to take in the excitement of the *Centenario*. She joined a half million or more people who lined the capital's elegant boulevard, the Paseo de La Reforma, to watch the parade of marching soldiers and floats depicting the high points of Mexican history. But King and other onlookers sensed bitterness tempering the joy of the event. Mexico was in turmoil. The tremendous gap between rich and poor created a tension one could feel like the rumbling of a volcano about to erupt.

In the middle of the parade was a coach bearing President Porforio Díaz. September 15 was the president's eightieth birthday, and the parade honored that event as well as the *Centenario*. The crowd fell into a strange hush when people saw their leader. Many Mexicans blamed Díaz and his dictatorial policies for the fearfulness gripping the country. An American observer noted, "Thousands thronged to watch the passing show, yet there was no outburst of delight. Porfirio Díaz, brilliant with royal decorations and distinguished guests, swept by without applause."

From Laredo, Texas, Francisco Madero issued a proclamation declaring November 20, 1910, to be a day of rebellion. He urged Mexicans to take up arms, overthrow their leaders, and arrange for new elections. November 20 came and passed with no great armed struggle rocking Mexico. Villa shot up a troop train in the state of Chihuahua, but it was impossible to tell whether he was acting as a revolutionary or as a bandido.

In Zapata country, all was quiet as a truce had settled on the disputed fields. For the moment, Zapata's followers worked the soil free from hacienda interference, but always the men kept their rifles and other weapons nearby.

Despite the relative peace in Morelos, much of Mexico was on edge. Grinding poverty plagued the country, from the factories and railroad yards in the north to the farms in the south. Even the upper classes, fearing revolution, were open to a change of leadership. It was true that Porfirio Díaz had brought order to the land and that this was a relief compared to the chaos of the past. But now that sense of order seemed about to break down. More and more Mexicans listened to the man who began to rise in stature as a new national hero—Francisco Madero.

Francisco I. Madero

Madero reentered Mexico at the border town of Ciudad Juárez in the spring of 1911. President Díaz sent troops to the city with orders to arrest the upstart Madero. A pitched battle broke out between federal soldiers and rebels commanded by Pancho Villa, who was determined to protect the revolutionary leader. Villa displayed the bold tactics and courage that would make him famous in battles to come, as he led his men down city streets with pistols blazing. In well-fortified areas, Villa ordered his followers to break into houses. Once inside, they used picks to knock down the walls of the adjacent house and enter that one too. In this manner—house by house and street by street—Villa and his band advanced.

On May 11, 1911, the commander of the Ciudad Juárez garrison, General Juan Navarro, surrendered. Villa stood Navarro up against a wall and was about to execute him. This same General Navarro had ordered rebel prisoners to be bayoneted during an earlier skirmish, and now Pancho Villa sought revenge. Just before the command to fire, Francisco Madero intervened. He told Villa to stop the execution because shooting war prisoners was a savage act. A shouting match ensued between the two men. According to one story, Villa pulled out his pistol and aimed it directly at his chief's face. Madero, according to the story, said words to the effect of, "Go ahead, shoot." Then Villa, moved by Madero's courage, broke down and wept. Villa finally shook his leader's hand and canceled the execution.

Mexican revolutionaries identified closely with their leaders. The followers of Villa in the north came to be called the Villistas while Zapata's men in the south were referred to as the Zapatistas. Porfirio Díaz believed that the Villistas were the greater immediate threat, and he sent the bulk of his soldiers to the north. This gave Zapata and the southern rebels a chance to strike.

The American View

Americans living in the Texas town of El Paso sat on their rooftops and watched the swirling street battles taking place in Ciudad Juárez, which lay just across the Rio Grande. Reports say that El Paso men bet on which side would win, as if the war for the city were a football game. The U.S. government took a less sporting view of the disorder shaking its southern neighbor. American investors owned oilfields, cattle ranches, and factories in Mexico. To protect American interests, Washington sided with the Díaz government because it represented security. As a safe measure, President William Taft ordered 20,000 troops to patrol the frontier. Porfirio Díaz, and even many Madero supporters, denounced the troop transfer as another example of the Americans bullying their weaker neighbor to the south.

The Zapatistas controlled the countryside while the hacendados and federal soldiers occupied the cities. In early 1911, the hacendados hired more guards and added to their supplies of guns and ammunition. Zapata watched the hacienda arms build-up with alarm. He believed his men were too poorly trained and equipped to confront the hacendados in open battle, but he had to act before enemy garrisons became even stronger.

In April 1911, the Zapatistas approached the ancient town of Yautepec, which was protected by local police and federal soldiers. There they employed a secret weapon—the "dynamite boys." These were boys chosen because they were quick on their feet and made small targets. Also, they looked innocent and, it was hoped, could approach the fortified town without drawing fire. American newspaper writer H. H. Dunn witnessed the battle and gave this account:

> Suddenly [once inside the town], the little fellows reached inside their ragged shirts. They withdrew small, round, bright objects, tin cans with a short piece

of string dangling from each. The boys touched these strings to the burning ends of cigars, then hurled the round, bright objects at the *cuartel*—guard-house. Two threw their cans on the tiled roof. Four pitched them in to the narrow windows, from which the muzzles of machine guns peered. The boy at the center threw his toy into the open door. All ran. . . . A section of the roof rose in the air. The great door leaned forward, split down the center, and fell. The two guards disappeared [in the blast]. . . . Fragments of other men came through the gaping doorway. . . . A human head came through a window, bounced, rolled across the road and into the plaza.

The main Zapatista force lay in hiding on the outskirts of town while the dynamite boys did their deadly work. Thundering explosions triggered by the boys were the signal for all to rush forward and conquer Yautepec. This early battle was a harbinger for the courage and tenacity with which the Zapatistas would conduct revolutionary war.

As the revolution developed in Morelos, Zapata journeyed from village to village seeking soldiers for his small army. Campesinos heard of his bravery and the spirit possessed by his warriors. Gradually, Zapata became a legend. An elderly Indian woman from the town of Milpa Alta recalled:

The first we knew of the Revolution was one day when the great Zapata arrived. . . . Señor Zapata stood up in front of his men and spoke to all the people of Milpa Alta: 'Join me! I have risen up; I have risen in arms . . . we don't like what the rich pay us. It's not enough to clothe or feed us. I want all the people to have their land; then they can sow and harvest corn, beans, and other grains. What do you say? Will you join me?'

The town of Cuautla proved to be one of Zapata's toughest battles in 1911. On the surface, the rebels enjoyed strength in numbers. Zapata commanded 4,000 farmer/warriors and prepared to challenge about four hundred federal soldiers. But these were crack troops, members of the famous Fifth Calvary Regiment, nicknamed the "Golden Fifth." The cavalrymen were armed with rifles and machine guns, and they were well trained for siege warfare. Zapata's campesino army fought with a few ancient rifles and with farm tools, including machetes and rakes.

The Battle of Cuautla raged for six days and six nights in May 1911. According to one witness, they were "six of the most terrible days of battle in the whole Revolution." Much of the fighting was hand to hand, pitting federal bayonets against Zapatista machetes. Hatred and passion ruled the warfare. Zapata discovered that one of his most difficult tasks was to restrain his followers from charging senselessly into machine gunfire. The Zapatistas took no prisoners. Federal troops who tried to surrender were gunned down. The intense battle provided a preview as to how the Revolution in the south would be fought—without mercy and with no rules bringing even a trace of civility to the battlegrounds.

The final triumph at Cuautla launched the career of a man who would become the most feared and certainly the cruelest of all the Zapatistas. In the height of battle, Felipe Neri, one of Zapata's best subcommanders, hurled a dynamite bomb toward a window. The bomb hit a wall, fell at his feet, and exploded. Neri suffered multiple injuries including the complete loss of his hearing. Deafness made this mean man even meaner. In the future, he tortured prisoners without the burden of having to listen to their screams. Sometimes he cut the ears off of captives as if to avenge his battle-induced deafness. In the gory lore of the Revolution, Neri was referred to as *mochaorejas*, a "clipper of ears."

A string of victories sent Emiliano Zapata's reputation soaring among revolutionaries in the south. From miles around came leaders of smaller rebel groups who wanted to join the Zapatistas. They reasoned that Zapata's men had to be the greatest fighters in the south because they had defeated the best force Díaz could send against them. Even in the elegant Cuernavaca Hotel, the Bella Vista, Rosa King heard glowing tales about "the wily Zapata and his constantly growing bands of untrained Indians."

In August 1911, Emiliano Zapata married Josefa Espejo, the daughter of a wealthy cattle dealer. His courtship and marriage was traditional and met the standards of a Mexican gentleman. Zapata had asked Josefa's father for her hand, but he was turned down because the father reasoned that young Emiliano did not own enough land to be a proper provider for his daughter. When the father died, the couple entered into marriage. They married in a Catholic church, with the ceremony and exchange of vows meeting the approval of the local priest.

Beyond his marriage ceremony, Zapata's conduct with females would certainly not be approved by a priest or the Catholic Church. Zapata was a womanizer, the type of man who believed he required the love and affection of many women. Ladies were attracted to him because he was handsome, well mannered, and always perfectly dressed. He returned their attention with zeal. He had several wives and many girlfriends, and he fathered at least six children. Little is known about his wives and girlfriends, as they stayed in the background most of the time.

With battles storming in the north and south, President Díaz locked himself in his Mexico City office. Even there he found no sanctuary. Every day crowds gathered at the Zocalo, the large plaza in the city center, and shouted up to the president's window: "Death to Díaz! Death to Díaz! *Viva la Revolución!*" Such demonstrations were rare under the Díaz dictatorship. One rainy night federal troops, unused to

The Zocalo, the main square in the heart of the
historic center of Mexico City

dealing with unruly crowds, panicked and opened fire. People looking from windows counted two hundred dead bodies sprawled about the Zocalo, their blood mixed with rainwater.

On May 21, Díaz sent an emissary to Madero calling for a cease-fire in the war being fought in the north. The president offered to resign his office and give Madero free access to the capital. He sent no agents to speak with Zapata, but months later he said to an associate, "I was calm until the south rose." Several days after the cease-fire, Díaz—now looking like the elderly man he was—boarded a train to the port city of Veracruz. Before leaving the capital, he said, "They [the revolutionaries] have loosed the wild beasts—let us see now who will tame them." A ship took Díaz to exile in France, where he would die four years later.

An excited Mexico City waited for the arrival of the country's new leader. Finally, after thirty-five years of rule by an absolute dictator, change had come to Mexico. Men and women shouted, "*Viva Madero! Viva la Revolución!*" For a breathless moment, it seemed that the warfare stage of this revolt was over. Then, almost at the moment Madero stepped off the train in Mexico City on June 7, 1911, a tremendous earthquake jarred the capital. Buildings crumbled and dozens of people were killed and injured. Many believed that the earthquake was a message from God warning that Mexico was condemned, that the death and destruction of the Revolution was destined to go on and on.

Francisco I. Madero arriving in the city of Cuernavaca on June 12, 1911, for a meeting with Emiliano Zapata

CHAPTER 5

The Plan of Ayala

A leading citizen of Cuernavaca rushed into the Hotel Bella Vista shouting, "Quickly close everything, *Señora* King! The fierce Zapata is coming." In desperate tones, he urged the English hotelkeeper to leave town, adding, "[Zapata] is killing and destroying everything in his path."

After the fierce Battle of Cuautla, Zapata gained a dual image: To the compesinos of the south he was an angel, sent from heaven with the special mission to protect them. To the Mexico City newspapers, which were read by the middle classes everywhere in the country, he was a half-crazed, fiendish man who delighted in committing wanton murder.

Rosa King decided to judge for herself the merits of this controversial figure. Standing on her hotel's front porch, she first saw Zapata and his revolutionaries. "No Caesar ever rode more triumphantly into a Roman city than did the chief, Zapata," she said. King described Zapata's followers as "a wild-looking body of men, undisciplined, half-clothed. . . . But they rode in as heroes and conquerors, and the pretty Indian girls met them with an armful of bougainvillea and thrust the flaming flowers in their hats and belts."

Zapata could have stayed at the Bella Vista, but he chose not to do so. Perhaps the price of a room at King's hotel was beyond his budget. Also, he had work to do. Francisco Madero had invited him to Mexico City for a conference, and he wanted to prepare for this important meeting. His attitude toward Madero was one of wait and see. Characteristically, he never rushed into a new course of action. Once he made up his mind on a certain plan, his devotion to that plan was absolute. Still, he preferred to study and think out a proposal before making a first step.

A document that he and his aides examined carefully was Madero's Plan of San Louis Potosí, which provided a blueprint as to how he would act as president. The Zapata camp liked what it saw regarding land disputes. In the plan, Madero wrote, "Through unfair advantage taken of the law . . . numerous proprietors of small holdings, in their majority Indians, have been disposed of their lands . . . by courts of the Republic. It being full justice to restore to the former owners the lands of which they were disposed of so arbitrarily."

This was legalistic language, but it said exactly what Zapata had believed all along: the government, through the courts, had illegally taken land. Now the logical course of action would be to return the land to its rightful owners.

Madero and Zapata met for the first time on June 8, 1911. The conference took place in the elegant Madero family mansion on Berlin Street in Mexico City. From its start, the discourse between the aristocrat and the campesino leader was uncomfortable. Zapata asked about land reform as spelled out in the Plan of San Louis Potosí. Madero changed the subject and told Zapata that the Revolution was over and therefore it was time to disarm his followers. Once more Zapata brought up the land question, and again Madero demanded that the Zapatistas lay down their weapons.

Emiliano Zapata had a flair for the dramatic. He believed in acting things out when words failed to deliver a point. Zapata's biographer, Octavio Paz Solórzano, described what next took place in the future president's mansion: Zapata rose, held his rifle in one hand, and with the other hand pointed to Madero's gold watch. Zapata said:

> Look, Sr. Madero, if I—able to do it because I am armed—take your watch away from you and keep it, and if, as time goes on, we happened to meet again, and both of us are carrying the same weapons, would you have the right to ask me to give it back. . . . Well that is exactly . . . what has happened to us in the state of Morelos, where a few hacendados by force have taken over village lands. My soldiers (the armed peasants and all the villagers) insist that I tell you, with all respect, that they want you to move immediately to restore their lands.

The lesson transmitted by this scene was clear. The armed campesinos demanded the return of the land that was stolen from them, and only by keeping their arms would they have the power to enforce their demand.

Paz, Father and Son

Octavio Paz Solórzano was a Mexico City lawyer who supported revolutionary causes and at one point served as Emiliano Zapata's secretary. His more famous son, Octavio Paz Lozano (1914-98), was a poet, historian, and diplomat. Paz Lozano wrote Mexican history in glowing terms without glossing over his country's frequent twists and turns into violence. He once called the Mexican Revolution of 1910-20 a "fiesta of bullets." In 1990, Octavio Paz Lozano won the Nobel Prize for Literature.

Madero was not yet president when he met Zapata in June 1911. He was clearly the country's most popular leader and could have just assumed the office. But in his view, Mexico had already had too many chiefs who picked up the mantle of leadership without the benefit of elections. One of his major promises was to bring free and honest elections to Mexico, and he intended to honor that vow. Elections were scheduled for October 1911. In the meantime, the country was governed by interim president Francisco León de la Berra, an old Porfirio Díaz ally.

Mexico remained tense as the country awaited the election date. Zapata continued his program of taking over disputed hacienda land and ordering people to farm it and defend it with bullets if necessary. Some newspapers in this pre-election period portrayed Zapata as a wild-eyed radical or even a communist who opposed private property of any kind. However, Zapata insisted only that land recently and unlawfully absorbed by the haciendas be returned. When a writer asked him what he thought of communism, he answered, "Explain to me what it is."

To no one's surprise, Madero won the presidency in October by a huge majority of votes. It was the most honest, open election ever held in Mexico. In the past, Díaz had ordered jail inmates to mark ballots and then send them to vote-counters. Madero's victory spelled an end to bogus elections. Now—at last—Mexico had a legitimate president.

One afternoon shortly after the election, Rosa King heard rifle fire cracking outside. Tensely, she looked out her hotel window. To her relief, she saw federal troops near the town square saluting their new commander by firing rifle shots into the air. At the center of the soldiers, an officer sat on a splendid horse. "He sat as though made of iron, without a motion of his body, his face without a smile."

The officer was General Victoriano Huerta, a man known and feared in military circles for his cunning and his cruelty. President Madero had chosen Huerta to pacify the troublesome rebels in the south. Negotiations with their leader, Emiliano Zapata, had reached a painful stalemate. Madero insisted that the southern revolutionaries turn in their firearms before he would discuss land reform; Zapata refused to order disarmament until all the stolen land was returned. Madero believed he had no choice but to fight fire with fire and bullet with bullet. So he gave the command of the south to General Huerta, who had his own ideas about putting down rebellion.

Huerta led his armies out to capture or kill the Zapatistas, who he called a band of "ridiculously pretentious bandits." The troops burned villages and murdered peasants who they believed were sympathetic to the revolutionaries. This violence triggered an unexpected reaction. As Huerta stepped up his campaign of terror and bloodshed, hundreds of campesinos flocked to join Zapata's ranks. Emiliano Zapata became god-like in the hearts of the country people.

Hundreds of rural soldiers, or *el rurales*, like these pictured here joined Zapata.

During his campaign against the Zapatistas, General Huerta lived at the Bella Vista Hotel in Cuernavaca. Increasingly, the hotel guest list was made up of high-ranking military officers. Rosa King said of Huerta's stay at her hotel, "He . . . drank heavily and nearly every evening had to be led off to bed." During the day, he rode at the head of his troops, destroying village after village. Still, he had no success in finding the elusive Emiliano Zapata. Finally, President Madero dismissed Huerta from command of the southern forces. The president simply did not trust the general. King wrote, "Huerta was very, very angry [at the dismissal] and . . . swore revenge on Madero. He felt he had been made a fool of."

All his life, Zapata had been moved by Bible stories. He regarded the act of betrayal, such as Judas's denunciation of Christ, to be the darkest and most terrible sin one could commit. Now he believed that by refusing to return stolen campesino lands, Madero had betrayed his own Plan of San Luis Potosí and the Revolution as well. Zapata's last letter to Madero warned, "You can begin counting the days, because in a month I will be in Mexico City with 20,000 men and I will have the pleasure of . . . hanging you from one of the tallest trees in [Chapultepec Park]."

Historic Chapultepec Park in Mexico City

For Zapata, it no longer mattered who led the nation—Díaz, de la Berra, or Madero. All were tools of the rich. None would grant the campesinos their basic rights. It was time for the Revolution to take a new direction, one dedicated to the poor and to the landless.

With his customary love of drama, Zapata called for a meeting of campesino leaders in November 1911. As firecrackers popped and a small band played the Mexican National Anthem, Zapata stepped out of a mountain hut. Some reports said he had the Mexican flag draped around him like a cloak. Standing before an audience of about one hundred campesinos, Zapata read out the Plan of Ayala. Written in the town of Ayala with the help of Otilio E. Montaño, his schoolteacher friend, the plan contained Zapata's ideas for building a new Mexico. It became Zapata's manifesto and his way of fighting the Madero government with both pen and sword.

The Plan of Ayala attacked President Madero for his broken promise to carry out land reform. The word *traición* (betrayal) was used five times. However, the Plan was far more than a condemnation of the president. It called for the immediate restoration of land illegally acquired by the haciendas. Also, up to one-third of the land owned by the plantations could be taken and given to small farmers, providing that the plantation owner was compensated for the loss. Finally, and perhaps most important, the plan stated that this land policy should be applied not only to Morelos but to all of Mexico.

The Plan of Ayala did not embrace radicalism or communism. In fact, it was similar to President Madero's own Plan of San Luis Potosí. Its policies would not cause the haciendas to disappear from the Mexican scene. Instead, the Plan of Ayala contained a vision of Mexico as a land of independent small farmers. Some one hundred years earlier, Thomas Jefferson had similar aspirations for the infant United States.

In bitter terms, the Plan of Ayala demanded Madero step down from his office: "[We] declare . . . Francisco I. Madero inept at realizing the promises of the revolution . . . because he has betrayed [its] principles. . . ." The plan called for General Pascual Orozco, a northern revolutionary leader, to take over the government, "and in case he

Francisco I. Madero, Mexican political leader, with hand in sling

[Orozco] does not accept this delicate post, recognition as Chief of the Revolution will go to General Don Emiliano Zapata." The Plan ended with the words: "Mexican people, support this plan with arms in hand and you will [promote] the prosperity and well-being of the fatherland."

At first, President Madero ignored the Plan of Ayala. He read the document and noted its many instances of bad Spanish grammar and misspellings. Madero urged a newspaper to publish it "so everyone will know how crazy that Zapata is." But Madero consistently underestimated Zapata and his popularity with the common people. The Plan of Ayala was written in a passionate language that the campesinos readily understood. Conversely, Madero's Plan of San Luis Potosí was worded for lawyers and had to be carefully explained to the uneducated farmer.

Zapata often told his followers, "You must never ask, holding a hat in your hand, for justice from the government of tyrants, but only pick up a gun." With this sentiment in mind, Zapata launched a guerrilla war in Morelos in early 1912. Small bands of his followers raided haciendas and made off with horses and firearms. Often the defeated hacienda owner was compelled to give a "loan" of cash to the Zapatistas. During the guerrilla raids, the Zapatistas fought with stunning courage, as if death held little meaning to them. The fighters were buoyed by another saying frequently shouted out by their leader: "Men of the south! It is better to die on your feet than to live on your knees!"

The bloody raids brought cries of protest echoing from the Morelos planters to the nation's president. Madero was accused of being too soft, too liberal to make a tough stand against the revolutionaries in the south. The president was a vegetarian, and some critics said his meatless diet robbed him of natural aggression. He found himself caught

Guerrilla Warfare

A small force waging hit-and-run raids on a larger body of troops is said to be fighting a guerrilla war. The term originated in the early 1800s when the mighty French army under Napoleon occupied much of Spain. To resist the occupation, Spanish patriots launched "little wars" against the French. The word for war in Spanish is *guerra*, and a little war is a *guerrilla*. It is pronounced *gurr-ee-aa* in Spanish but sounds a lot like *gorilla* in English.

The Emperor Napoleon in His Study at the Tuileries, an 1812 painting by Jacques-Louis David

between forces on the left (the Zapatistas) and those on the right (the hacendados), both of whom demanded that he step down and give way to a more effective leader. A frustrated Madero grew to believe that Zapata was his most serious enemy. That man, in the president's mind, was an uncompromising rabble-rouser who had to be eliminated for the sake of his nation's peace.

In early 1912, a new army officer, General Juvencio Robles, checked in to Rosa King's Cuernavaca hotel. He had been appointed by President Madero to take command in the south and crush the Zapatista rebellion. King noted that Robles possessed a certain charm. On the morning of her birthday, he directed the military band to play the traditional song "*Las Mañanitas*" under her bedroom window. But Robles had an unpleasant habit of bragging about how intense and cruel the war against the Zapatistas would become under his authority. When King expressed shock concerning the general's plans, he said, "Now, now, *señora*. . . . You are only a woman and you do not understand these things. Why, I am trying to clean up your beautiful Morelos for you. . . . [And] if they [the Zapatistas] resist me, I shall hang them like earrings to the trees."

Mexican soldiers riding horses during the Revolution,
as depicted on a wall painting in Cancun, Mexico

CHAPTER 6

Land
and
Liberty!

President Madero declared martial law in Morelos in the spring of 1912. By announcing martial law, the president gave the military even greater freedom to deal with the "upstarts" and the "bandits" who were so disrupting the country. The new commander in the south, General Robles, regarded martial law as a license to imprison and kill. Dozens of suspected Zapatistas were lined up and shot without the benefit of a trial. Said one farmhand, "If they found you walking, they would shoot you. If they found you working, they would shoot you. That was what they called martial law."

The Zapatistas blended in with the civilian population. They were never an organized army, being part-time soldiers and part-time farmers. While assuming their roles as farm workers, they responded vaguely and even played dumb when questioned by the army. "Who is this fellow Zapata? Maybe I know him. Maybe I don't." This ruse might or might not save the skin of the campesino, depending on the whim of the arresting army officer.

Two of Emiliano Zapata's generals

The "uniform" of the Zapatistas consisted of simple homespun farm clothes. Practically every farm worker in the south wore the same garments—white cotton pants and shirt and a broad-billed straw hat. The cotton clothes made working under the hot sun bearable. Since they were so common, the "country whites" helped the Zapatistas maintain their disguise as simple farmers. But when called to battle, the cotton-clad soldiers swooped down upon haciendas shouting "Land and Liberty!" Those words—*Tierra y Libertad!*—were a war cry echoed by revolutionaries in all parts of Mexico.

Hacienda owners employed small armies of guards to defend their holdings. As the Zapatista campaign intensified, bloody battles were fought at the hacienda walls. The fighting often had a nightmare quality. One hacendado who defended his property with particular vigor was captured and nailed to the plantation gate. The federal army resisted the Zapatistas with martial law—meaning no law at all—on their side. Many young men were shot simply because they were of military age and therefore could someday join the Zapatista forces.

Once a hacienda was conquered, Zapata distributed the land to campesinos based on their past claims. Some hacendados avoided being raided by paying "protection" money to guerrilla army commanders. Zapata and fellow officers considered the protection money to be a tax. In this manner, Zapata financed the revolution in the south.

True to his vow to Rosa King, General Robles made a spectacle of hanging captured Zapatistas, or anyone else he believed supported the guerrilla bands. King wrote, "Those of the rebels he caught, General Robles strung up on trees, where their companions could see them, and the passengers on the trains that passed that way. My daughter and I often saw the sickening sight of bodies swinging in the air. At that high altitude they did not decompose, but dried up into mummies, grotesque things with the toes hanging straight down in death and hair and beard still growing."

General Robles also imposed a program of forced relocation on the country people of Morlelos. He assumed, as did President Madero, that all the peasants of the south were Zapatistas at heart. One of Robles's colonels explained to Rosa King, "The only way we can quiet down Morelos is to ship out these Zapatistas. If we break up families doing it—well, our families have lost their husbands and fathers too."

Throughout southern Mexico in early 1912, troops entered villages, rounded up men, women, and children, and marched them to the nearest railroad station. In Cuernavaca, a horrified Rosa King watched the residents of an entire town, including some people she knew, being forced onto trains. She wrote: "Never shall I forget the sight of those poor wretches standing tied together, not one uttering a word. . . . The soldiers were hustling [them] into a cattle boxcar, pushing them in till there was not even standing room. They boarded up the doors and nailed them shut."

Trains took the uprooted campesinos far to the south. There, if they survived the trip without food or water, they were sold to coffee and lumber plantations. More than one hundred years earlier, Mexico had outlawed slavery, yet the relocated farmers were slaves in every manner but the name. Many failed to return to their old homes because they were worked to death or they perished from hunger or disease.

Despite this harsh treatment, no one in Morelos betrayed Emiliano Zapata. His base camp remained a secret. The names of his high-ranking officers were never told to federal authorities. In fact, the despair felt by the people drove them to join Zapata's forces. One farmhand recalled, "I said to myself, 'Rather than [let the soldiers] kill me . . . I'd better get out of here.' And so I went to war along with the Zapatistas." Rosa King noted, "The savage persecution by the Federals . . . turned the Zapatistas into fighting demons."

Zapata kept in hiding and moved often while forced resettlement and wholesale executions ravaged the campesino communities. As a fighting general, Zapata longed to wage open warfare, dreaming of the day when he could launch large-scale battles against the federal army and drive it from Morelos. But Zapata lacked trained soldiers, proper rifles, and—especially—ammunition. Bullets came from suppliers in the north, and army roadblocks kept them from delivery to the Zapatistas. Zapata had no choice but to continue guerrilla warfare until his military position improved.

Even peaceful campesinos were regarded as enemy guerrilla fighters. Said General Robles, "All Morelos, as I understand it, is Zapatista . . . there's not a single inhabitant who doesn't believe in the false doctrines of the bandit Emiliano Zapata." Troops under Robles even arrested Zapata's mother-in-law, sister, and two sisters-in-law. The women were accused of trumped-up charges and held in a Cuernavaca jail. Zapata was known for his courage. Robles undoubtedly hoped that Zapata would launch a bold operation to rescue the women from the heavily guarded jail, and his men would kill the rebel chief in the process. Zapata refused to take the bait.

The civil war raging in Morelos was a confusing conflict with no clear-cut sides. Often a person caught in the middle of the warfare could not determine just who constituted the enemy. Morelos teemed with bandit gangs who robbed and killed in the name of revolution when in fact the gangs were interested in plunder alone. Also, not all revolutionary guerrilla groups acted under Zapata's direct orders. Several rebel leaders in the south commanded their own armies and were only loosely allied with Zapata.

One such semi-independent chieftain was Genovevo de la O, an ex-charcoal maker who knew every dark recess in the forested Morelos mountains. Using today's terms, de la O would be condemned as a terrorist. His specialty was laying dynamite under tracks and blowing up trains. Mostly he targeted troop trains, but he did not hesitate to destroy passenger vehicles and killing civilian travelers.

Hatred bred hatred in the Moreles civil war, and one atrocity always called for an avenging atrocity. To stop de la O's campaign against the railroads, federal troops stormed his home village of Santa Maria. Soldiers doused the peasant houses with kerosene and set them ablaze.

Among the bodies later recovered from the ashes of Santa Maria was that of de la O's young daughter. De la O extracted revenge by stepping up his attacks on trains and killing scores of passengers.

As the violence escalated, Zapata tried to keep the actions of his own followers under control. He had a sense of his public image, and he did not want his soldiers to be labeled as bandits or fiends. In a letter, Zapata warned his lieutenants, "The better we behave, the more support and aid we will have among the people, and our triumph will come more quickly." Yet senseless bloodshed remained a part of life in the south. Since Zapata was the most famous leader in the war zone, the press blamed him for the attacks on trains and the wanton killings going on in the south. The Mexico City newspaper *El Imparcial* came out with the headline, "Zapata Is the Modern Attila." The paper compared Zapata to Attila the Hun, the barbarian who once had battled the Roman army. After that headline, the press often referred to Zapata as the "Attila of the South."

A 1913 photograph of Genevevo de la O

Unrest in Morelos frightened President Madero. He never envisioned himself as a wartime leader, and the pressure of making military decisions took its toll. An American reporter, observing the Mexican president, wrote, "He was greatly changed . . . a dozen years had been added to his apparent age. . . . He showed loss of sleep and was extremely nervous, with the impatient manner of a man who is trying to do too many things at once."

Toward the middle of 1912, Madero backed measures designed to pacify the south and possibly bring Zapata to the peace table. The president appointed a new governor for Morelos, Francisco Naranjo, a northerner and a political liberal. Madero canceled martial law in the state. As another gesture of goodwill, he dismissed the hated General Robles, replacing him with enlightened army commander General Felipe Ángeles. Finally, in the fall of 1912, Zapata's relatives were released from the Cuernavaca jail.

Zapata dismissed the peace feelers coming from Madero. He remained true to his Plan of Ayala, which called for Madero to step down before talks could even begin. Zapata was a complex man of rather simple revolutionary faith. Rigidly carrying out a stated program was his strength as well as his weakness. From the campesino point of view, his stubborn pursuit of the Plan of Ayala principles made him a noble leader. Yet it seemed in 1912 that President Madero genuinely wanted peace in the south and was willing to make concessions. Perhaps at least talking to the president would avert bloodshed. Zapata refused even to whisper the word *compromise*. He announced, "Not until Madero's downfall will we enter into peace agreements."

The demands written out in the Plan of Ayala were Zapata's only policy. Late in the year 1912, the level of violence diminished somewhat in Morelos. At harvest time, most of Zapata's troops had to return home and turn to farm chores. Zapata led bands of guerrilla fighters and harassed haciendas by burning crops. He also attacked smaller army units in hopes of seizing their rifles and adding to his precious supply of bullets.

In Mexico City, President Madero found himself doubly damned. He stated he was willing to discuss land reform, and he was damned by the large landowners as a weakling who was caving in to the rebels. He never supported a set of laws that would institute a program of fair land redistribution, and therefore he was damned by Zapata and the campesinos as a tool of the rich. Toward the close of 1912, his presidency was increasingly in peril.

Political rivals in Mexico City sensed that Madero's government would soon fall, and they moved to take over in his wake. Chief among the rivals was Felix Díaz, the nephew of disposed dictator Porfirio Díaz. Secretly, Felix Díaz made a deal with ambitious army general Bernardo Reyes to execute a coup d'état and seize the presidency. Díaz knew that many wealthy Mexicans sought the law-and-order society once imposed by his famous uncle. He hoped to restore such rule and gain the support of the upper classes.

On Sunday morning, February 9, 1913, a formation of several hundred troops marched into the Zocalo in downtown Mexico City. The plaza was filled with churchgoers walking to services at the National Cathedral, which rose on the Zocalo's north side. The soldiers were commanded by General Bernard Reyes. He planed to force his way into the National Palace (the seat of government), depose President Madero, and replace him with Felix Díaz. The operation was expected to be quick and bloodless because it was based on the element of surprise. However, Gustavo Madero, the president's brother, was informed of this coup d'état by his own spies. Gustavo lacked his brother's idealism and his naivety. He believed he was better able to deal with the hard edge of Mexican politics.

The column of troops reached the center of the plaza when a shot rang out and the leading officer fell from his horse. An explosion of rifle and machine gun fire crackled over the ancient plaza. Churchgoers screamed, ran, and were struck down by the hail of bullets. Gustav Madero's own loyal soldiers lay hidden in the National Palace, shooting from the windows. In the crossfire, two to three hundred innocent citizens were killed. Also killed was General Reyes, who commanded the operation.

Mexican historians call what followed the *Decena Tragical*, the Ten Tragic Days. For ten days and nights, the forces of General Díaz fought the forces loyal to Madero. It was largely an artillery duel that took

The Metropolitan Cathedral in the main square in Mexico City. Built over more than two centuries, between 1573 and 1813, it is the largest and oldest in the Americas.

place in the heart of the crowded city. Civilians lay huddled under mattresses as artillery shells tore into the buildings and houses. The death toll of the tragic days was far greater among civilians than it was for soldiers.

Far from this urban battlefield, intrigue decided the fate of Mexico. General Huerta hated President Madero and longed to be president himself. Huerta made a deal with Felix Díaz that would allow him to become president until new elections could be arranged. Both parties assumed the elections would be rigged to allow Díaz to win. Privy to this deal was Henry Lane Wilson, the ambassador from the United States. Ambassador Wilson regarded Madero as a madman and was eager to see him overthrown. The secret agreement was later called the Pact of the Embassy because most of its details were made within the United States Embassy building.

Mexico for the Mexicans

During his thirty-year reign, President Porfirio Díaz allowed foreign firms to build up huge companies in Mexico. Díaz reasoned that foreigners had capital and greater management experience than did Mexican businessmen. Under Díaz, foreign investment flowed into Mexico: Spaniards purchased coffee plantations in the deep south, Englishmen owned oil fields near Tampico, and Americans bought up the railroads. These outsiders made fabulous profits because they paid low taxes to the government and because Mexican workers earned a pittance compared to what the foreign owners would have had to pay help in their native lands.

Diplomats such as Henry Lane Wilson lobbied the Mexican government to pass laws favorable to foreign business interests. Critics claimed Wilson and his staff practiced "dollar diplomacy." Naturally, Mexicans resented what they perceived as a sell-out of their resources. Another battle cry heard frequently during the Mexican Revolution was "Mexico for the Mexicans."

While the artillery shelling in the city continued, General Huerta's agents sprang into action. President Madero, his brother Gustavo, and Vice President José María Pino Suárez were arrested. After the arrests, the guns fell silent. Mexico City residents, dazed and shaken, emerged to the rubble of their streets and discovered that their president was in jail and General Victoriano Huerta now led the nation.

The men guarding Gustavo Madero threw him to a group of drunken Huerta soldiers who were celebrating their victory. The soldiers beat him savagely and then shot him, although not fatally. This left President Madero and Vice President Pino Suárez still alive and in jail. Certain that her husband would soon be killed, Mrs. Madero appealed to the only person she thought could possibly help—Henry Lane Wilson. The American ambassador reluctantly agreed to grant an audience with Madero's wife. When Mrs. Madero asked him to intervene and save the life of her husband, he said, "That is a responsibility that I do not care to undertake, either for myself or for my government."

General
Victoriano
Huerta

Near midnight on February 22, 1913, Francisco Madero and Pino Suárez were put in separate cars and driven to the city limits. In pitch darkness, the two were pushed outside their cars and shot. The army reported that the president and vice president were killed while attempting to escape custody. Two days later, Ambassador Wilson cabled the American State Department: "I am disposed to accept the [Mexican] Government's version of the affair and consider it a closed incident."

Henry Lane Wilson

On the night that Madero and Pino Suárez were murdered, Huerta was at a party with Henry Lane Wilson at the American Embassy. It was George Washington's birthday, and the two men, who often drank together, toasted the father of Wilson's country. Several weeks later, the incoming American president, Woodrow Wilson (no relation), fired Ambassador Wilson because he suspected that the American diplomat had a role in Madero's downfall. Henry Lane Wilson returned to his native Indiana, where he died in 1932, always maintaining he had served with dignity and honor when he was the American ambassador to Mexico.

Mexico now had a new dictator in Victoriano Huerta. Unlike Madero, who at least had a few loyal supporters, this chief was distrusted by the rich because of his history of treachery. He was also hated by the poor, who viewed him as a cruel tyrant. With Huerta in charge, the Mexican Revolution surged forward into a new stage of bloody civil war.

Soldiers loyal to Emiliano Zapata attack General Victoriano Huerta's federal army at Morelos in 1913.

CHAPTER 7

Battling a President

Emiliano Zapata was fond of saying, "I can pardon those who kill or steal because perhaps they did it out of need. But I never pardon a traitor." He looked upon Victoriano Huerta, the self-proclaimed president of Mexico, as a traitor of the worst order because he betrayed the ideals of the Revolution as well as his own country.

Huerta, in turn, despised and feared Zapata. He viewed Zapata as a dangerous influence on the campesinos, a man who would lead the poor to revolt and upset the order of Mexico. Shortly after taking power, Huerta delivered a speech before a group of Morelos hacendados. These were the people whom he hoped would support his presidency with money. Huerta warned the planters to prepare for a bitter war in the south: "It is necessary to clean out all such people [as the Zapatistas], and you must not be surprised if perchance something abnormal happens, for the [present] state of affairs calls for procedures that are not actually legal but which are indispensable for the national well-being."

To enforce his get-tough policy, Huerta sent General Juvencio Robles, the old scourge of the south, to Morelos with orders to capture or kill Zapata. He also reimposed martial law. Huerta told Robles to rule Morelos "with an iron hand and disdaining womanish contemplations."

Zapata and his followers remained safe in secluded camps in the mountains of southern Mexico. No maps marked these regions. They were known only to isolated farmers. None of the rural people, even when subjected to torture by the army, revealed the location of the Zapatista outposts. "Here even the stones are Zapatista," said one resident. It was impossible for Robles to wage war on the Zapatistas because he could not find them. With no Zapatista army to fight, General Robles instead made war against the Morelos people.

Once more, resettlement was enacted and thousands of compesinos were stuffed into railroad cattle cars. Many young men were taken to Mexico City, where they were forced to serve in the federal army. Women, children, and the elderly were transported to the south to become slaves on the plantations. Many died of suffocation because they were packed so closely in the cars. Those who passed on did so standing up. They remained on their feet in death, for there simply was no room in the cars to fall.

War and forced resettlement scarred the face of what was once an extraordinary, beautiful state. Villages that had existed for two hundred years became ghost towns. Routinely, the federal army burned a village after herding its people onto trains. The Zapatistas, in turn, burned hacienda fields. A traveler to Morelos said that "the state was only a rough sketch of what it was two years ago . . . now [it is] converted into a sad heap of ashes, the monotony of the burned fields interrupted only by one or another deserted hamlet also half ruined by fire."

With so many heads of families and community leaders missing, moral authority disappeared in campesino villages. Gangs of starving children, ten and twelve years old, looted markets and robbed people. One of the most feared gangs of looters was made up of women and headed by a one-time tortilla maker named La China (meaning "the curly-haired woman"). These women were known for their brutality;

even tough chieftains such as de la O and ferocious ear clipper Felipe Neri stayed out of La China's path.

Still, the campesino ties with the Zapatistas strengthened. Villages posted sentries on roads. When federal soldiers were seen approaching, an alarm sounded and the villagers rushed to the nearest Zapatista camps, where they knew they would be protected. Rosa King, who remained in Cuernavaca through much of Huerta's rule, wrote, "The government made every effort to paint the Zapatistas as monsters and so whip up feeling against them, but . . . we realized these wild men had a spirit [the federals] lacked. For good or evil, they were united by a passionate faith in their leader, Zapata, and Zapata followed a vision—land and liberty for his people—and let nothing stand in his way."

As his home state was being terrorized, Zapata launched a limited offensive. On April 17, 1913, he attacked the town of Jonacatepec, which was guarded by a federal force of about five hundred men. After a battle that lasted thirty-six hours, the town fell and the Zapatistas collected three hundred cavalry horses, several machine guns, and thousands of precious bullets.

The supply of bullets remained a glaring Zapatista weakness. By 1913, General Zapata (as he was now called) had confidence in his soldiers. The men were both brave and well disciplined. He believed his followers would now prevail in an open battle with the federals. But battles often lasted two or three days, and during that time the Zapatistas could expend 20,000 or more rifle rounds. Never did Zapata enjoy a sufficient supply of ammunition. As much as he wanted to shift from guerrilla warfare to conventional warfare, his supply situation prevented the change.

While Huerta held power in Mexico City, his enemies ruled much of the remainder of the country. The mountains and deserts of northern Mexico were the realm of Pancho Villa, the bandit turned revolutionary. Also in the north was Venustiano Carranza, a wealthy cattle dealer of European descent who at one time supported Madero. Carranza believed he—and only he among the revolutionary figures—had

A 1917 photograph of Venustiano Carranza

the experience, breeding, and education to be president of Mexico.

The other major northern commander was Álvaro Obregón, an exschoolteacher and a passionate student of history and military science. Collectively, the northern leaders were called the Constitutionalists because they wished to restore the country's 1857 constitution. Also, they demanded that Huerta step down. Beyond the constitution and the ousting of Huerta, the northern leaders agreed on nothing. In fact, they distrusted each other, and each one looked for the opportunity to destroy his rivals.

Ultimately, the Constitutionalists in the north provided relief to the suffering campesinos of southern Mexico. With revolutionary fighting increasing in the north, Huerta had no choice but to transfer his main forces from Morelos to the northern regions. The despised general Robles was also transferred. At last a breath of peace swept over the south of Mexico.

Zapata used the respite to reorganize his army. Many long-term and trusted followers were made sergeants. Zapata's forces acquired a new name: the Liberating Army of the Center and South. General Zapata centralized his authority, gaining greater control over formally independent chieftains such as de la O. Zapata's brother, Eufemio, advanced in the officer's ranks, although Emiliano still worried about his brother's destructive drinking habits. In a major reorganization move, soldiers from far-flung bands were told that in the future they must obey the orders of officers from any other Zapatista unit. This policy of centralizing authority brought greater cohesion to the Liberating Army of the Center and South.

Felipe Neri, the notorious ear clipper, was a casualty of the new and reorganized Zapatista army. Neri used brutal tactics to compel the *pacificos* (the peaceful ones) to support his forces. *Pacificos* were poor villagers who did not wish to choose sides in the Revolution. Zapata preferred to leave the *pacificos* alone since they did no harm; Neri demanded their loyalty or else. In a letter, Zapata said he had to watch Neri closely because "left to himself this man is very disorderly." Neri fumed at any restrictions put on him, and he reminded Zapata of his sacrifices in the past: "Even though I find myself without the use of my ears, I serve you as no one else has." In January 1914, Neri

Felipe Neri, in 1915

was killed in a gun battle with an offshoot Zapatista force. General Zapata made no official comment about the killing. The dreaded earclipper was now out of his life.

The status of women rose among the Zapatistas. Traditionally, Mexico was a man's world where women were confined to kitchen duties, the care of children, and service to the church. The Revolution brought changes to these old patterns. At first, women associated with the revolutionary forces were wives or girlfriends of the male soldiers. They forged for food, cooked, and washed clothes for their men. Many carried babies on their backs as they worked. Then, when the man was killed in battle, the woman picked up his rifle and joined the fighting ranks. Women soldiers (*soldaderas*) fought in Pancho Villa's army, although he disapproved of the practice. Among the Zapatistas, women became officers and leaders.

Emiliano Zapata said little about the promotion of women within his army. Practice alone allowed the women to gain promotions. If a female proved herself worthy on the battlefield, she was given a leadership role.

Rosa King praised the contributions of Zapata's *soldaderas* and scolded the upper-crust women who denounced them as mere camp followers: "I bow in respect of this [soldier] class—the class despised by women of indolent wealth. . . . The Mexican women who marched with the Mexican soldier . . . [did] their part in laying the foundation of this liberal government of to-day."

Machoism and the Role of Women

Today, women serve as governors, mayors, and senators in Mexico. Laws exist forbidding discrimination based on sex, but such laws are recent developments. Mexican women did not even gain the right to vote in presidential elections until 1958.

Over the years, the practice of machoism has held women back in Mexican society. Machoism—even the word is controversial since many Mexican males insist they never think or behave in a macho manner—is a code of conduct that requires men to lead in matters of government and the family. Some historians say that Mexican machoism is rooted in colonial times when Spanish men pushed native men aside and took Indian women as wives and girlfriends. Mexican males adopted a macho, or super manly, code to make up for this historical humiliation.

In his book *The Labyrinth of Solitude*, Octavio Paz writes, "It is impossible not to notice the resemblance between the figure of the macho and that of the Spanish conquistador. This is the model—more mythical than real—that determines the images the Mexican people form of men in power: *caciques* (tribal chiefs), feudal lords, hacienda owners, politicians, generals, captains of industry. They are all *machos*. . . ."

Intellectuals freely joined the Zapatistas. Communism was a popular belief among intellectuals of the time, and numerous outsiders thought the Zapatista movement was communistic in nature. Anarchism (the belief that government itself is hurtful to common people) was also a concept entertained by many intellectuals. Emiliano Zapata, though never a communist or an anarchist, was fascinated by the intellectuals who drifted into his camps. Intellectuals were more concerned with ideas than action, and therefore they would seem distasteful to a military man such as Zapata. But Zapata respected educated people who were versed in literature and poetry.

One intellectual he embraced was Manuel Palafox, an engineer who was short, was said to be "spidery," and was loaded with energy. Palafox wrote articles and essays that he hoped would be picked up by newspapers. The articles disclaimed the image of Zapata as the "Attila of the South" and showed instead the positive side of the Zapatista movement. Palafox told of the hundreds of campesinos who were displaced and made homeless by warfare but found food and safety in Zapatista camps.

Richard Flores Magón

The slogan "Land and Liberty," which was adopted by the Zapatistas, came from the intellectual writings of Ricardo Flores Magón, a widely read Mexican anarchist. Born to a poor family in 1873, Flores Magón established the Mexican Liberal Party, which promoted socialism and opposed the presidency of Porfirio Díaz. He was forced to flee to the United States, where he joined leftist groups and spoke against American involvement in World War I. In 1918, he was accused of violating American espionage laws and sentenced to twenty years in prison. He died in Leavenworth Prison, Kansas, in 1922. Before his death, his slogan "*Tierra y Libertad!*" emerged from the Zapatista camps and was used as a battle cry by all revolutionary armies. Today, Flores Magón, though little known outside the country, is hailed as a martyr by Mexican radicals.

Zapata and his intellectual comrades sent letters to the United States asking that country to recognize the Zapatistas as the legitimate government in Mexico. This was tricky business because it ran contrary to the Plan of Ayala, Zapata's golden rule book. The original plan gave leadership of the nation to Pascual Orozco, the northern revolutionary leader who was once allied with Madero. In 1913, Orozco joined up with Huerta, and Zapata cursed him with the worst criticism he knew—that Orozco was a traitor. According to language in the Plan of Ayala, with Orozco out of the picture, national leadership should fall to him, Emiliano Zapata. From the beginning of the struggle, Zapata maintained he did not want an office in the post-revolutionary government of Mexico. Now, words in his own Plan of Ayala compelled him to take such an office. This was a dilemma that Zapata never planned to face. As it turned out, circumstances never compelled him to take a high position in official government.

Hollywood and Zapata

In 1952, the movie *Viva Zapata!* was released to theaters in the United States. The film starred acclaimed actor Marlon Brando as Zapata. The script was written by revered novelist John Steinbeck, and Academy Award-winning Elia Kazan served as the director. It was a suspenseful and action-packed movie and a hit with moviegoers in the U.S. and Mexico. However, the film shows Zapata becoming Mexico's president, and this never happened. Emiliano Zapata, in real life, shunned all offers to accept a national office.

A scene from *Viva Zapata!*

Zapata failed to gain respect or recognition from leaders in the United States. To the Americans, he was another wild-eyed revolutionary in a disorderly and increasingly dangerous country. American newspapers often printed stories from the Mexico City newspapers that painted a sinister picture of the Zapatistas. Many Americans came to believe that Zapata was both a communist and a fiendish killer.

Huerta tried to legitimatize his government by holding elections in October 1913. The elections were a farce, as the process was hopelessly rigged in Huerta's favor. The only one who could provide opposition was Félix Díaz, the ex-dictator's nephew. But Díaz, believing he was next on Huerta's assassination list, fled the country. Huerta won the October election handily and later appointed his friends and cronies to positions in Congress.

Though Huerta called himself president of the nation, Mexico City was the only place in the country where Huerta's rule was unchallenged. He ran the capital with an iron hand, as his agents and secret police arrested anyone who dared speak a negative word against him.

Huerta's grip on the country was strengthened, temporarily at least, by the actions of American president Woodrow Wilson. The American chief believed that the upheaval in Mexico threatened U.S. interests, and as long as Huerta held power the fighting and disorder would continue. Through a network of spies, Wilson learned that a German ship was steaming toward the port city of Veracruz, bringing a load of machine guns and other arms to Huerta's army. In April 1914, Wilson ordered the U.S. Navy and Marine Corps to seize Veracruz. A wild gunfight broke out between the Marines and Mexican military school cadets, who valiantly tried to defend their city. When the smoke of battle cleared, some two hundred young Mexican cadets lay dead on the streets of Veracruz.

Outraged, President Huerta called upon his countrymen to fight this "Yankee invasion." He declared, "In the port of Veracruz we are sustaining with arms the honor of the nation." Nothing riled a Mexican patriot more than bullying by its powerful northern neighbor. The Veracruz occupation charged Mexicans to put aside their differences and unite against the Yankee imperialists. Mobs stormed American-owned buildings in Mexico City, throwing stones and breaking windows. American flags were torn off poles and burned.

Yankee Imperialism

Mexicans never forgave or forgot the Mexican American War of 1846 to 1848, which saw the American government taking over what had been the territory of northern Mexico. This territory later became Texas, the southwestern states, and California. The land grab was a humiliating chapter in Mexican history and triggered deep resentment toward the richer nation to the north. Americans were loosely called Yankees, and any incident of American interference in Mexican affairs was branded as "Yankee imperialism."

Zapata fumed when he was told of the Veracruz invasion. "I felt like my blood was boiling," he said. But Zapata determined that Huerta was Mexico's most immediate enemy, and most of his countrymen agreed. It was easy to see through Huerta's scheme: he tried to shift the blame for Mexico's woes onto the Yankees. Blaming an outside force for internal problems was a common tactic by a dictator. The tactic failed. Mexicans were led by a president most of them despised, and Huerta's days in power dwindled.

The hammer blow for Huerta came in March 1914, when Pancho Villa led 8,000 warriors into the fortified town of Torreón. The battle was fierce as the Villistas faced dug-in artillery. Villa, who was never seen without at least one pistol in his belt, personally led all the major attacks. American newsman John Reed marveled, "His method of fighting is astonishingly like Napoleon's . . . Villa is the Revolution. If he died, I am sure that the Constitutionalists would not advance beyond Torreón in a year."

Pancho Villa and the Americans

In the early years of the Revolution, many Americans lauded Pancho Villa as a hero, a Mexican Robin Hood. Villa carefully cultivated his folk hero image to the Americans. Like Robin Hood of old, he stole from the rich and fed starving villagers. But he made sure he distributed food to the poor while American news writers and photographers were present to record the event. The American-owned Mutual Film Corporation paid Villa $25,000 to make an action-packed movie based on his life. The film, *The Life of General Villa*, opened in 1914 and thrilled American audiences.

In July 1914, Victoriano Huerta resigned as president and quietly took a ship to Cuba. Millions of pesos in the Mexican Treasury disappeared with him. Huerta had led the nation for sixteen months of almost constant warfare. He died in Texas in 1916 of cirrhosis of the liver, a disease associated with alcoholism.

With Huerta gone, the federal army collapsed, leaving Mexico City open to the revolutionaries. Pancho Villa wanted to be first in the capital, but all the armies of the north were dependent on train travel and therefore also dependent on coal. Venustiano Carranza, who now called himself the First Chief of the Revolution, blocked Villa's coal shipments. Villa swore revenge on the treacherous First Chief.

On August 15, 1914, a Constitutionalist army commanded by Álvaro Obregón marched into Mexico City. Days later, Venustiano Carranza made his triumphal entrance to the capital. The two Constitutionalist leaders assured Mexico City residents that the Revolution was over and law and order would be restored. Carranza spoke with confidence because he had the support—although it was lukewarm support—of the United States. President Wilson determined that Carranza, more so than the other revolutionaries, was best able to defend American business interests in Mexico.

American forces in Veracruz left the port on November 23, 1914. Before sailing, the Americans gave the Constitutionalists a cache of weapons and supplies, including rifles, machine guns, 3 million rounds of bullets, and 632 rolls of barbed wire. This gear was intended for the armies of Carranza and Obregón, and it would prove vital to the Constitutionalists in the very near future. The commander who received the military supplies was Cádido Aguilar, Carranza's son-in-law.

A monument remembering the battle and
defense of Veracruz City on April 21, 1914

Carranza had organized a convention to meet in the city of Aguascalientes and form a post-revolutionary government. The convention was set up in such a way as to name Carranza president of Mexico when the Revolution was finally resolved. But in a shocking development, convention delegates swung the other way and favored Zapata and Villa.

At the Aguascalientes convention was thirty-year-old lawyer Díaz Soto y Gama, one of the intellectuals who attached himself to the Zapatista movement. Soto y Gama was a socialist and an admirer of anarchist writer Ricardo Flores Magón. Zapata instructed Sota y Gama to argue for the Plan of Ayala, but the lawyer had a habit of wild talking.

American ships at Veracruz in 1914

Sota y Gama began a speech at the convention by naming all the great leaders in world history: Jesus Christ, Buddha, and Karl Marx, and he included Zapata in this list. Soto y Gama then grabbed the Mexican flag and cried out, "What's the good of this dyed rag. . . . How is it possible, gentlemen of the Revolution, that for a hundred years we have been venerating this silly mummery, this lie?" The convention hall exploded in shouts and curses. These were military men who revered their country's flag as they did the Holy Cross. Several delegates put their hands on their pistols. Soto y Gama later explained that he simply used the flag as a symbol to explain the importance of the Plan of Ayala. Tempers cooled, but the speech almost started a riot.

Changed Views

After the Revolution, Díaz Soto y Gama remained a leading figure in Mexico as a socialist, a leftist lawyer, and a journalist. In his old age, however, he did a political about-face and became a staunch anti-communist. During the Cold War, he praised the United States for resisting the communist Soviet Union. He died in Mexico City in 1967 at the age of eighty-seven, still preaching against communism.

The armies of Carranza and Obregón moved east of Mexico City to regroup and prepare for a new stage of revolutionary fighting. Carranza's departure meant that once more the capital was an open city. From the north came the forces of Pancho Villa, and from the south marched Zapata and his followers. The people of Mexico City were thrown into panic. So far they had had little contact with revolutionary armies. Newspapers told them that the rebel forces were made up of fiends whose leaders were madmen. Now these barbarians were at their gates.

Of the two revolutionary groups, the capital residents reserved their greatest fear for the Zapatistas. They were a mostly Indian army led by a dark-skinned mestizo. From the time of the Spanish conquest, the Mexico City upper classes dreaded the outbreak of a race war. The terrible prospect loomed that Indian peoples, infuriated by hundreds of years of near enslavement, would take their revenge on whites. As Zapata and his followers approached the capital's southern suburbs, wild rumors spread from household to household: the Zapatistas practiced Aztec human sacrifice rituals. They delighted in torture—crucifying people on telephone poles and staking them over hills of man-eating ants. Stores and restaurants in Mexico City locked their doors. Even police stations closed. Those who could escape the capital did so. But the vast majority of the city-dwellers had no choice but to wait for the arrival of the Zapatistas. They prayed and lit candles to saints while believing they were doomed.

Pancho Villa, seated in the presidential chair, with
Emiliano Zapata, on his right, in Mexico City

CHAPTER 8

Villa and Zapata

Zapata's troops entered Mexico City in late November 1914. No military bands heralded their arrival. None of them wore a uniform. They did not look like an army. Instead, they were simple country men and women who came from the south in groups of a dozen or more. They walked on sandals—although many were barefoot—and they wore their white farm clothes, which fit like pajamas. Most appeared to be awestruck as they beheld the palatial homes and tall buildings of a big city for the first time in their lives.

The Zapatistas had no commissary to keep them supplied with food and other necessities. In the south they had been fed by the locals, and in return they had offered the local people protection. Here, in Mexico City, the Zapatistas were forced to ask residents for food. A young Mexico City man remembered being approached on the street by a group of Zapatistas. Rifles hung from their shoulders and machetes from their belts. The young man was terrified. But the leader of the group asked politely, "Young master, would you let us have a little paper money [in order to buy food]?"

With no tents to serve as housing, the Zapatistas slept in the open air in the Zocalo and other plazas. There were no public toilets available for them to use. The men and women soldiers relieved themselves in the plazas, much to the disgust of Mexico City's higher classes. Still, Mexico City residents were impressed by these polite and humble country soldiers. The only serious incident came one night when a fire engine with a clanging bell sped past a Zapatista camp. The farmers, never having seen such a vehicle before, opened fire, killing and injuring a dozen firemen.

Several days after Zapata's men arrived, the Villistas entered the capital. They came on trains whose boxcars were riddled by bullet holes from previous battles. The Villistas were a larger and better-equipped army. Their commissary was well supplied, and they had no need to beg for food. At first, Villa's men behaved reasonably well, limiting their celebrations to wildly firing their rifles in the air.

The Church and The Revolutionaries

The two armies held starkly different views concerning the Catholic Church. The Zapatistas carried banners showing pictures of the Lady of Guadalupe, the patron saint of Mexico. They stopped in front of churches and dutifully made the Sign of the Cross. The Villistas, by contrast, showed no such respect. Some of them even looted churches. Perhaps the attitudes of the two groups reflected their leadership. Zapata, though he rarely attended Sunday services, claimed to be a serious Catholic. Villa generally denounced religion. "I believe in God but not religion," the rebel chief often declared.

Villa and Zapata agreed to meet on December 4, 1914, in the town of Xochimilco, about twelve miles south of the capital. The town was decorated with flowers to celebrate the occasion. Villa later remembered, "So many were the bouquets and wreaths . . . [that] our horses were walking on them while we rejoiced in our hearts." Schoolchildren assembled in the plaza and sang songs to the two leaders.

Zapata took his eight-year-old son, Nicolás, with him to the meeting. Nicolás was one of Zapata's favorite children. Zapata probably hoped the boy would be thrilled by the festivities in the plaza and the importance of the get-together with Villa. But Nicolás slept through the whole affair.

A conference, the very first between Villa and Zapata, took place at noon in the Xochimilco schoolhouse. American agent George Carothers observed the talks and wrote a detailed report to President Woodrow Wilson. He noted that the two men made "a decided contrast." Villa was "tall, robust, weighing about 180 pounds with a complexion as florid as a German." Carothers described Zapata as dark-skinned and a "thin faced" man, "weighing probably about 130 pounds." The American detected an atmosphere of tension as the two sat "in an embarrassed silence, occasionally broken by some insignificant remark."

The only subject they agreed upon was that the Constitutionalist leader, Carranza, had betrayed the Revolution. Villa said it was because Carranza was wealthy and in the future they should not trust "men who have always slept on soft pillows. How could they ever be friends of the people, who have spent their whole lives in nothing but suffering?"

Those revolutionaries who expected a grand alliance to emerge from the Xochimilco meeting were disappointed. While Zapata and Villa conversed in a friendly manner, it was clear the two were wary of each other. Zapata looked upon Villa as a man hungry to gain power, and he believed the goals of the Revolution had already been badly compromised by ambitious people. Also, this meeting suggested that warfare would continue as both chiefs viewed Carranza as a dangerous enemy.

All differences were put aside for a great fiesta to be held on Sunday, December 6, a celebration designed to mark the triumph of the Revolution. During the evening of the 5th, the Villistas and Zapatistas got together to party on the Mexico City streets. Guitars and accordions were produced, and the two revolutionary groups traded songs. They were different people. The Villista northerners were ranch hands and coal miners; the Zapatista southerners were dirt farmers. Almost all of them had grown up in poverty, and they were veterans of countless battles. Now many held the happy—if naive—belief that the Revolution was over and at last the weary warriors could go home.

The Revolution and Its Music

The Zapatisas and the Villistas operated hundreds of miles from each other, so it was natural for the two armies to favor different songs. A favorite among the Zapatistas was a sad song that told of the damage the war had done to their lovely state of Morelos:

> Our pueblos only plains
> White ashes, pictures of horror
> Sad deserts, isolated places
> Where only sorrow stirs.

The Villistas and other northern armies sang "*La Cucaracha*," the lively tune about a dizzy cockroach that does not know where he is going. One verse in "*La Cucaracha*" pokes fun at the slightly overweight Pancho Villa: "One thing makes me laugh / Pancho Villa with no shirt on."

December 6, 1914, dawned bright and crisp as the two armies assembled for a grand parade into the heart of Mexico City. Villa's army, the Division of the North, numbered 35,000, all dressed in khaki uniforms. Some 20,000 members of the Liberating Army of the Center and South, clad in country whites, completed the marching formation.

Leading the parade, of course, were the two famous generals: Pancho Villa and Emiliano Zapata. Thousands of Mexico City residents lined the sidewalks to watch. "How the young ladies showered us with flowers!" wrote Villa. Zapata, ever the dandy, wore a tight-fitting charro suit and rode on a magnificent white horse. Villa, who was usually casual in his dress, donned a dignified blue suit for the occasion. At one point, a breeze blew Villa's cap off his head. Without breaking his horse's stride, Zapata reached to the ground, picked up the hat, and handed it to Villa. Zapata prided himself at being an athletic trick rider, and this stunt with the hat proved he had not lost his touch.

The parade ended at the Zocalo, where the principals dismounted and entered the National Palace, the seat of government. Once inside, Villa pointed to the presidential chair, which symbolically stood as the throne of Mexico. He sat on the chair and grinned for cameras. Then he rose and invited Zapata to sit down. A hint of anger overcame Zapata as he said, "I didn't fight for that. I fought to get the lands back. I don't care about politics. We should burn that chair to end all ambitions."

Zapata and most of his followers left Mexico City on December 9 and returned to the south. His meeting with Villa had been discouraging, and his experience in the capital left him troubled. Unlike his soldiers, Zapata had been to the big city before and he was not awed by the buildings and grand boulevards. Now that he had fought through a revolution, he saw the capital as the core of power, a dark and sinister power that was holding back his people. He also missed life in the country. Earlier, he had pointed to a city sidewalk and remarked to Villa, "The men who have worked and walked the hardest are the last to get any good from these sidewalks. And I'm speaking for myself. When I walk on a sidewalk, I feel like I'm going to fall."

Zapata and Villa departed with handshakes and friendly gestures. The gestures were a mask hiding their mutual distrust. The two never met again.

Villa and his army remained in the capital for weeks after Zapata left. At this point, in December 1914, Mexico had no effective government. A caretaker president, General Eulalio Gutiérrez, was theoretically in charge. But Gutiérrez had little actual authority. He did not even command his own police force. The Aguascalientes convention had split up days earlier, its delegates still torn in debate. The country was leaderless, and Mexico City was potentially a lawless place.

Pancho Villa (seated, left), Eulalio Gutierrez (seated, middle), and Emiliano Zapata (seated, right) together for a banquet at the National Palace in 1914

After their initial spell of civil behavior, the Villistas went on a rampage by looting stores, robbing people, and spreading terror. Liquor stores were their favorite target. After the men got drunk, their violence turned ugly. The terrible crime of rape was committed in all parts of the capital. Villistas grabbed women and raped them on public sidewalks as horrified onlookers watched. Men who tried to stop the attacks on women were gunned down. Pancho Villa himself added to the carnage when he raped a refined Frenchwoman who managed a hotel. This crime was reported in the world press, and Villa's once-shining image as a Robin Hood was forever tarnished.

In Morelos, Zapata and his followers found a moment of peace. The Zapatistas never were an army; they were instead an insurgent people. Now, in the south, they built what was in practice a separate nation.

The nation within a nation was an agrarian society with an economy based on small farms. The farms were carved out of hacienda land, and Zapata himself created many of the boundaries. He drew on old records, and he interviewed elderly people to determine the borders of the small milpas as they had existed before the haciendas expanded. Typically, one farm was separated from a neighbor's farm by a stone wall. Zapata called upon engineers to survey the land and build the walls, but he cautioned them: "The villagers say that this stone wall is the boundary; you're going to draw the line along it for me. You engineers often care a lot about straight lines but the boundary is going to be this stone wall, even if you have to work for six months measuring all the ins and outs."

The Zapatista army remained a force comprised of farmers first and soldiers second. The Zapatistas tilled the soil with rifles slung on their shoulders, as they could be called to war at a moment's notice. Beyond the campesino army, Morelos had no state police force. Village counsels were charged with keeping order.

A mural of Pancho Villa on horseback, on display at the Historical Museum of the Mexican Revolution in the city of Chihuahua, Mexico

On the village level, Zapata acted with the skills and grace of a popular politician. He was an honored guest at wedding and baptismal parties, always joking with the women and drinking with the men. He provided clothing and food to widows and to destitute elderly people. He took particularly good care of the families made fatherless by revolutionary warfare. When traveling from town to town, he always made sure he had enough money in his pocket to comply with any reasonable request.

Zapata tried, as much as possible, to be gracious with former hacienda owners. One such hacendado was Ignacio de la Torre y Mier, who Zapata once worked for before the Revolution. Torre y Mier fell into Zapatista hands, and some sub-commanders demanded his execution. But Zapata remembered the hacendado as a fair man. Zapata released Torre y Mier from the jail where he had been held and told him he could roam free as long as he did not go beyond the boundaries of the town of Cuautla. Torre y Mier later fled from Morelos, some say with Zapata's secret help.

No one questioned that Emiliano Zapata was the ultimate leader over this realm. Under the stress of war, leaders tend to become larger-than-life heroes, and Zapata attained such a status. The man who was affectionately called 'Miliano was loved like a brother and obeyed without question as if he were an Aztec king. In the south, he served as president and as chief judge.

Under Zapata's orders, four sugar mills were rebuilt and began operating. The people ran an armaments factory, a large shop where men rehabilitated old rifles and manufactured bullets. At another shop, silver was melted down and silver coins produced. Morelos silver minted by the Zapatistas was the only currency of real value produced in revolutionary Mexico. Villa's army traveled with its own printing press and issued paper bills with Villa's picture on the face. Merchants were forced to accept Villa's paper within the territories he controlled, but beyond those territories the bills were useless. The Zapatistas operated banks that gave loans to small farmers. Zapata said, "Now that there is money we must help those poor people who have suffered so much during the Revolution. It's very right that we help them because we still don't know what they might have to suffer in the future. . . ."

Zapata ordered his intellectuals, such as Díaz Soto y Gama, to organize a school system in his territory. Schools sprang up in villages that had never been served by a school before. Even night schools were established to teach reading and writing skills to illiterate adults. Soto y Gama and his associates did not tell the instructors in detail what to teach, but the teachers tended to be intensely loyal to their 'Miliano. Often the teacher told students that Emiliano Zapata was a saint sent by God.

Emiliano Zapata's advisor, Diaz Soto y Gama, a fiery
orator and one of Mexico's leading revolutionaries

Morelos citizens who had fled revolutionary fighting began to return. One of those drifting back was Rosa King, who had escaped to Mexico City when warfare spread almost to her hotel's doorstep. The Englishwoman's life had been a heroic odyssey. When she bought her Cuernavaca hotel, she spoke only a few halting words of Spanish, and she knew almost nothing of Mexican customs and traditions. Over the years, she mastered the Spanish language and brought her business through the harshness of a revolution.

As was true with other returnees, King was shocked to see what the war had done to the once lovely town of Cuernavaca. She wrote: "What a sight greeted us! Black, battered, bullet-pierced walls where had been comfortable, happy homes . . . everywhere signs of the dreadful conflict that had taken place. . . . My head had known that it would be like this, but my heart was not prepared." Her hotel was in shambles.

"Zapata Lives" is the message spray painted on a wall in present-day Mexico.

"The great dining room that had been my pride was bare—nothing left in it; only pigs and chickens living there together quite happily. The rest of the house was wreaked and ruined in the same degree."

As the days passed, King found her old hotel employees. These were once humble *pacíficos* with no interest in politics or government. She discovered that five years of revolution had resulted in changed attitudes. "I asked them about Zapata, and then, for the first time, I felt an eagerness, a kind of expectation stirring behind their guarded words. Little by little they brought out the tales of Zapata's prowess in battle, of his terrible just anger, and his goodness to the weak. . . ." One of her elderly female employees laughed when she remembered a plot cooked up by the hotel guest General Huerta to trap and kill Zapata. With a mocking smile, the woman said, "as though [Zapata] would be caught with snares like a common man, or killed in battle like anyone else."

This conversation left a deep impression on King. The country people of Morelos had come to believe that their leader, Emiliano Zapata, was immortal.

A 1910 photograph of two Mexican cavalrymen

CHAPTER 9

Fratricide

"What I can't get in my head is why we keep on fighting. Didn't we finish off this man Huerta?" So says a character in a famous novel of the Revolution, *Los de Abaho* (usually translated as *The Underdogs*). Around the country, Mexicans asked the same question. Leaders rose and fell, but the war went on ceaselessly. By 1915, the Mexican Revolution had become a force of its own, its fury gathering momentum like a round stone tumbling down a hill.

With the fall of dictator Victoriano Huerta, the war entered a confusing and dispirited general-versus-general stage. Villa's army fought for Pancho Villa and his ambitions. Carranza's army fought for the goals of the man who claimed to be First Chief. The revolutionary generals, who once claimed to be allies in the struggle against Huerta, now battled each other. Warriors still shouted the old battle cry— "Land and Liberty!"—but the words sounded empty. The principles that once guided the Revolution were forgotten in a whirlwind of fratricidal violence.

Zapata tried to keep his people out of the general-versus-general fighting by strengthening his separate nation in the south. Octavio Paz believed the society that Zapata developed was an attempt to recreate the Aztec kingdoms of the past. "Every revolution tries to bring back a Golden Age," wrote Paz, whose father served as Zapata's secretary. "The Zapatista movement attempted to rectify the history of Mexico and the very meaning of our existence as a nation. . . . The Zapatistas did not conceive of Mexico as a future to be realized but as a return to origins."

For the first half of 1915, the Zapatistas enjoyed a period of peace while warfare swept the north. Venustiano Carranza acted as if he were president of Mexico, though he had no legitimate claim to that office. However, he did have powerful supporters. Carranza was favored by the United States, and he had the blessings of the Catholic Church. But as long as revolutionary armies such as the Villistas and the Zapatistas opposed him, he knew his position was woefully insecure. Carranza decided to take on the Villistas first.

The Role of the Church

Mexico had been a Catholic country since the time of the Spanish conquest. Over the years, many individual priests labored passionately for the rights of the poor and for the Indians. Father Hidalgo and Father Morelos, both Catholic priests, were leading figures in Mexico's War of Independence. But high-ranking bishops in Mexico City generally supported those who resisted change. The Mexican Catholic Church enjoyed wealth and privilege. Church leaders longed to see men in political office who would safeguard their holdings. The Church had backed both Porfirio Díaz and Victoriano Huerta. Venustiano Carrranza was not zealous in his defense of the Church, but in 1915 the bishops supported him in hopes he would be their protector.

In April 1915, Álvaro Obregón led his army into a field outside of the city of Celaya. Obregón wished to be president some day, but he was willing to wait his turn. In the meantime, he willingly served as the chief commander of Carranza's Constitutionalist army. Obregón ordered his troops to dig trenches and roll out barbed wire. The general had studied reports about the terrible trench fighting taking place in World War I Europe. He learned how the comparatively new weapon, the fast-firing machine gun, had become a murderously efficient killing device when correctly deployed. Thanks largely to the United States, Obregón had machine guns. With machine guns, trenches, and barbed wire in place, the cornfields outside Celaya were transformed into a replica of a European fighting front.

General Obregón respected Pancho Villa as a courageous military leader, but he knew the man was also given to impatience and recklessness. Obregón commanded 11,000 troops for the coming battle while Villa led 30,000. The Constitutionalist general hoped these lopsided numbers would serve as bait and encourage Villa to attack his well-fortified front. Pancho Villa took the bait.

On the morning of April 6, 1915, bugles sounded amid shouts of "*Viva Pancho Villa!*" Headed by their leader, the Villistas charged their enemy's front lines. The result was death on a nightmarish scale. Obregón had laid out his machine guns to fire in precise crisscrossing lines. The Villistas were cut down before advancing even near Obregón's trenches. Celaya was the biggest and bloodiest battle of the Revolution. It was also the most one-sided defeat suffered by any army. When the smoke of battle cleared, some 4,000 Villistas lay dead and 6,000 were taken prisoner. Obregón had lost only about 150 men.

Weeks later, another Obregón-versus-Villa battle took place in the nearby city of Leon. In the height of fighting, an artillery shell hit General Obregón, tearing off his arm at the elbow. Obregón was in such agony that he pulled out his pistol, pressed the muzzle to his chest, and pulled the trigger. The general reasoned that only death could ease his terrible pain. But earlier in the day, an assistant had cleaned his pistol and forgot to put a bullet in the chamber. The gun failed to fire.

A medal is pinned on General Alvaro Obregon. After he lost his right arm in the Battle of Celaya, he earned the nickname Manco de Celaya (the one-armed man of Celaya).

Obregón was rushed to a field hospital, where medics saved his life. His severed arm later became his badge of courage, as his political supporters claimed he had sacrificed the limb for Mexico's freedom.

After suffering the two stunning defeats, Pancho Villa retreated to the mountains of northern Mexico. He was no longer a factor in the general-against-general power struggle. Villa's absence gave Carranza the freedom to move south and eliminate Zapata and his farmer-soldiers.

In the summer of 1915, Carranza sent General Pablo González to the south with orders to conquer the Zapatistas. In his youth, González had been an unskilled factory worker who lived in poverty. He joined the army, and through sheer ruthlessness he rose to the rank of general and amassed a fortune. Despite his success, González was a laughing-stock within military circles. He was called the General Who Never Won A Battle, and the name fit. Even when he greatly outnumbered his opponents, his army always lost in the field. He had no mind for tactics and no ability to "read" a battlefield and let the lay of the land play to his advantage.

Zapata was aware of González's reputation as an incompetent officer, but he also knew of the disaster meted out against Pancho Villa in Celaya. So Zapata decided to avoid open battle with González, and he reverted once more to guerrilla warfare. Zapata divided his followers into units of one hundred and two hundred members. These small groups were ideal for lightning-quick raids on federal supply dumps, railroads, and small army units. Zapatista's main bases remained hidden in the deep and pathless mountains. General González, not being able to find the Zapatistas, waged war on the people of Morelos instead. He was painfully aware that he was the brunt of secret jokes told by rival commanders. He believed his military reputation could be saved in an instant if he arrested or killed the foxy Zapata.

González ordered all Morelos citizens to turn in their arms and warned of "the severest penalties" for failure to do so. To show he meant business, González had 225 prisoners he had been holding shot. Weeks later, he stormed into the town of Tlaltizapán, which had been Zapata's headquarters, and executed 286 residents, including 112 women and forty-two children. He reinstated the policy of forced exile, rounding up anyone even suspected of having Zapatista sympathies and driving them "like a herd of pigs" into railroad boxcars to be shipped to slave labor camps.

As was true in the past, the harsh measures only served to strengthen the peoples' ties to the Zapatistas. González offered huge rewards to anyone willing to give up the location of a Zapatista hiding place. He tortured suspects in the most horrible manner while seeking information. Still, no citizen of Morelos betrayed Zapata and his followers.

General Pablo Gonzalez and Jesus Carranza with their Artillerymen

Copr. R. Runyon.

General Pablo Gonzalez, fourth from left, and Jesus Carranza, far right, with their artillery in April 1914

Air Warfare

Flying in open cockpit biplanes, González's officers scanned the hills searching for Zapatista camps. These were the first aircraft ever seen in southern Mexico, and they created a shock. "One day I went to the fields . . . with another man," a Zapatista wrote years later, "and we saw something in the sky. What did we know about airplanes then! The plane . . . dropped two big bombs. How we were frightened!"

In November 1916 the Zapatistas blew up a train heading south from Mexico City. The enormous explosion took place so close to the capital that practically all the city's residents heard the blast. It was the deadliest train attack of the war, killing four hundred soldiers and passengers. General González was in Mexico City at the time, and in a rage he issued the order to all citizens of Morelos: "Anyone who directly or indirectly lends service to Zapatismo . . . will be shot by a firing squad with no more requirements than identification." The order also stated that anyone seen near railroad tracks "without satisfactory explanation" would be shot. A week later, as if to spite González, the Zapatistas blew up another train in the same area as the first blast.

Once more, González took his revenge on the people of the south. The war-weary citizens of Morelos suffered through a reign of terror imposed on them by a general who was hell-bent to improve his military reputation. González's troops rode from village to village shooting down small farmers and burning their fields and houses. The campesinos were near the breaking point. They were tired and didn't want to fight anymore. But when their loyalty was tested, the people met the test. In the hills and mountains, Zapata and his followers were invincible. Only the campesinos knew the secret lairs of the Zapatistas, and the campesinos willingly took these secrets with them to their graves.

Also exhausted was Englishwoman Rosa King. In early 1916, King tried to rebuild her hotel, but she was denied permits and building material. In desperation, she took her grievances directly to General Pablo González, who was based in Cuernavaca. In her book, she recorded what the general told her: "This is no time to talk of reconstruction, *Señora* King. The work of destruction is not yet completed. . . . I am about to destroy what still remains in Cuernavaca!" He went on talking, saying that there was no stamping out Zapata because all the towns and villages sheltered the Zapatistas. King shouted at him, "But our homes! Our property!" "Oh, *señora!*" he said. "That is of the past. That is all over. . . ."

To Rosa King, the message was clear: General González intended to destroy her future while at the same time crushing the Zapatistas. She believed her predicament was only fitting because she—a well-bred and educated Englishwoman—had become one with the people of Morelos. Therefore, she too was a Zapatista. Feeling the mysticism of the moment, she wandered to the edge of town, beheld the majestic mountains, and mused over the ancient inhabitants of this land:

> Rebelliously I called to them, 'Are you dead too?' Then voices came across the valley: voices of Toltecs and Chichimexans from their homes of centuries ago . . . voices saying, 'The very ruins all about you are telling you we live. Free-born men, like the mountains, will always survive. . . .' And then I knew I had not died. . . . I could feel that inside me my faith in creation's plan and humanity's cause still lived. . . . That was my relation to the Revolution.

For the rest of 1916, Zapata continued his aggressive guerrilla war. General González, despite the measures he imposed on the people, was unable to apprehend the rebel leader. In much of the country, the fighting between the generals raged on. Mexico bled.

In March 1916, Pancho Villa led 485 horsemen on a night march to the north. His unit crossed the international border and stormed into the town of Columbus, New Mexico. Shouting war cries and firing their guns wildly, Villa's men mowed people down, looted stores, and burned houses. Sixteen Americans were killed. Pancho Villa launched this raid largely because he was angry at U.S. President Wilson for recognizing the government of Carranza, his mortal enemy.

Villa, who was once a folk hero in the minds of Americans, was now condemned as a crazed killer. President Wilson sent a cavalry regiment under the command of General John Pershing into northern Mexico under orders to capture or kill Villa. But Villa knew every twist of every path in the mountains of the north, and he was always able to evade the American general. He became heroic in Mexican eyes because he outwitted the best general in the Yankee army.

In the fall of 1916, Carranza called for a convention to meet in the city of Querétaro and write a new constitution designed to replace the old document written in 1857. Carranza hoped to control the convention delegates and steer them into formulating a set of laws favorable to his views. But in a shocking development, the Querétaro delegates became charged with the spirit of the Revolution, and they wrote one of the most liberal constitutions ever created by any country.

The right of labor unions to form and conduct strikes was written into the set of laws. Using words similar to Zapata's Plan of Ayala, the constitution gave the government the power to seize excess lands owned by the rich and redistribute the lands to poor farmers. The constitution proclaimed freedom of religion, ending the centuries-old policy of Catholicism being the only religion allowed in Mexico. The new constitution became the law of the land on February 5, 1917. Carranza, deeply disappointed by its liberal tone, simply ignored the document.

Running virtually unopposed, Venustiano Carranza was elected as Mexico's president in March 1917. All Mexican states, with the notable

President Venustiano
Carranza, holding his hat

exception of Morelos, participated in the voting process. The separate society carved out by Zapata remained a region in rebellion. Zapata wrote Carranza a famous letter, calling him not president but "Citizen Carranza." The note was directed "[not] to the President of the Republic, whom I do not recognize, nor to the politician whom I distrust [but] to the Mexican, the man of feeling and reason, who I believe must be moved . . . by the anguish of mothers, the suffering of orphans, the worries and anxieties of the fatherland." In tough and blunt language, the letter asked Carranza "as a patriot and a man" to resign from his office. Carranza fumed and vowed to destroy the "Zapatista trash."

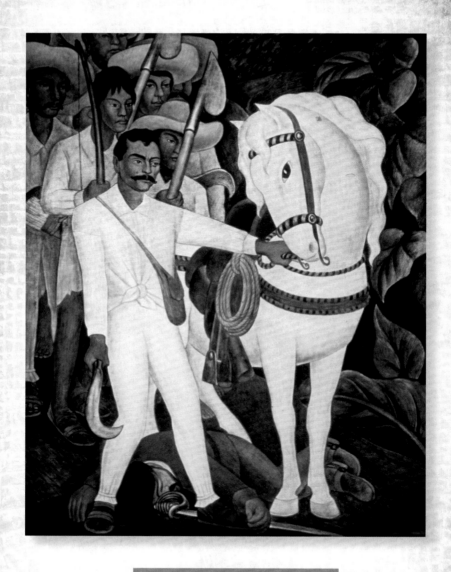

A 1931 fresco of Emiliano Zapata by Diego Rivera

CHAPTER 10

Twilight

In 1917 and 1918, the energy and fire of the Mexican Revolution diminished as the people were simply too weary to answer the call to arms. Villa remained in hiding in the north. Carranza consolidated his power in Mexico City. The American army under General John Pershing withdrew from northern Mexico in January 1917. World attention focused on Europe, where World War I raged. The United States entered the war in April 1917. With American armies involved in Europe, the threat of United States intervention in Mexico lessened.

The Zimmerman Note

A telegram written to the Carranza government helped prod the United States into entering the European war. In January 1917, a German government representative, Arthur Zimmerman, sent a telegram to Carranza suggesting that Mexico attack the United States through Texas and the southwestern states. Germany would support the invasion and Mexico could regain the territory it lost in the 1846-48 war. The British intercepted the telegram and published it in American newspapers. The proposal was little more than a harebrained scheme dreamed up by a minor German official, but it shocked the American public. The Zimmerman telegram, combined with Germany's aggressive submarine warfare, spurred the U.S. Congress to declare war on Germany on April 6, 1917.

Years of warfare left the once beautiful state of Morelos in ruins. Villages and farmers' fields had been burned, turning the land into a patchwork of weeds and black ashes. The war in the south was a war against the people as much as it was against the Zapatista armies. Hoping to starve the people into submission, federal troops shot cattle, uprooted fruit trees, and destroyed irrigation dams. Not even the property of the rich was spared, as soldiers looted and burned hacienda manor houses.

From 1910 to 1918, Morelos suffered a 25 percent reduction in its population. Citizens fled the state, were killed, or were removed in the forced relocation programs. Many villages were completely abandoned and stood as forlorn ghost towns. In small cities, starving stray dogs outnumbered people. Zapata entered Cuernavaca after a long absence and found the place "unrecognizable." In a letter to Octavio Paz Solórzano he wrote, "The streets and plazas have become dung heaps. The churches are wide open. . . . And the city has been abandoned because they took away all of the 'peacefuls' (*pacíficos*) by brute force . . . we found only three families in hiding."

Hunger was everywhere. With no field hands to tend crops, weeds infested even the hacienda grounds. Diseases such as malaria and typhoid fever broke out and claimed the lives of people already weakened by malnourishment. The worst of all maladies was Spanish influenza, which struck in 1918 and killed thousands in Morelos.

The Spanish Flu

The Spanish flu was a global pandemic that began in 1918 and killed 40 to 100 million people worldwide. More than 300,000 people in Mexico died as a result of the malady. The origins of the 1918 virus remain a mystery. But it was first reported by newspapers in Spain, and readers connected the disease to the country, despite influenza's presence in other places. It was spread through Europe largely by soldiers fighting in World War I.

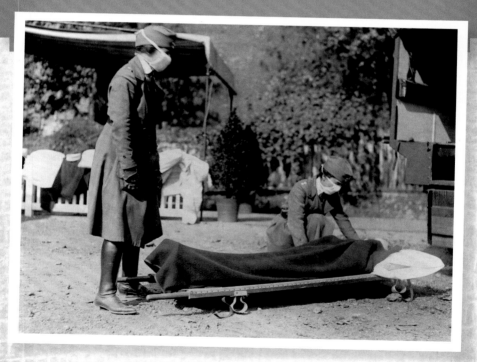

Two American Red Cross nurses demonstrate treatment practices in Washington, D.C., during the influenza pandemic of 1918.

A 1950s photo of a hacienda burned during the Mexican Revolution

No longer could the Zapatista army keep order in Morelos. Bandit gangs, some of them claiming to be Zapatista, raided small villages. With food shortages plaguing Morelos, the *pacificos* refused to share their meager supplies with the Zapatista army. Some Zapatista commanders simply took food from villagers. A gun battle broke out in the small town of Amecac when Zapatistas came to collect corn for tortillas. Men fell dead on both sides at Amecac, but it is believed

the Zapatistas suffered greater casualties. These battles for food took place contrary to Zapata's strict orders: "When asking for food you will do so with good words, and ask for it in a good manner, and always showing your gratitude. . . . The better we behave the sooner we will triumph and have all the [peoples] on our side."

Bickering broke out within the Zapatista ranks. Military officers believed that the intellectuals such as Díaz Soto y Gama were gaining too much influence over Zapata. Semi-independent officers began conducting their own military operations and ignoring Zapata's instructions. The commander himself grew nervous and edgy. One of his young officers wrote, "His [Zapata's] normally taciturn nature became dark, crabby, irritable, somewhat raw-nerved to such an extent that even men in his body guard feared when he called to them."

Zapata suffered a deep family loss when his brother was killed in a most horrible manner. For years, Eufemio Zapata had been an untrustworthy officer and a troublemaker in the Zapatista ranks. Eufemio drank heavily, got into barroom fights, and bullied fellow officers. In June 1917, he beat an old man with a stick because the man was drunk and annoying him. The man's son, Sidronio Camacho, was a high-ranking Zapatista officer. In revenge, Camacho, whose nickname was Loco (Crazy), shot Eufemio and then dragged his bleeding body over an anthill to let the ants finish him off. Many soldiers within the Zapatista army muttered that Eufemio "had it coming" because he had become such a destructive force. Emiliano Zapata said little about the gruesome killing. Sidronio "Loco" Camacho fled to Mexico City, where President Carranza gladly welcomed him into the federal army.

The Modern Zapatistas

In 1994, an armed rebel group took control of several townships in the Mexican state of Chiapas far to the south. The members called themselves the Zapatista Army of National Liberation. Comprised mostly of Mayan Indians, the modern Zapatistas sought to break away from Mexico and establish their own agrarian society. They linked themselves with Emiliano Zapata because they so admired his independence and dedication to a cause.

A Zapatista protest outside the National Palace in the Zocalo in Mexico City

Hoping to expand his movement, Zapata reached out beyond the farmers to the industrial workers and small shopkeepers. There were few factories in the agricultural state of Morelos, but those who worked in industry were badly underpaid. Zapata told the industrial workers that they had a common cause with the campesinos and suggested "that the calloused hands of the fields and the calloused hands of the factory grasp one another in a fraternal greeting of concord."

Feeling the Revolution drifting away from its original promise, Zapata tried to enter into alliances in order to shape a postwar future. He sent notes to Obregón, Villa, and Felix Díaz, who was organizing his own military unit far to the south. He even approached the United States through a businessman who was traveling in Morelos. In late 1918, after the European war ended, Zapata feared the U.S. would either invade Mexico outright or increase its support of Carranza. The United States never responded to his feelers. His search for allies within Mexico failed largely because revolutionary leaders refused to work in harmony with one another.

The alliance building and the reaching out to factory workers represented a growing worldview on Zapata's part. He had risen from a regional leader centered in Morelos to a national figure who sought security for all of Mexico. Perhaps if peace came to Mexico, a Zapata-led movement of workers and farmers would have formed and uplifted the nation's poor. But such a movement could only develop during peacetime, and Mexico, especially Morelos, remained at war.

Fear of the Spanish influenza temporarily kept the federal army out of southern Mexico. By late 1918, the pandemic abated and General Pablo González reentered Morelos at the head of 11,000 troops. Elections for a new president of Mexico were scheduled to take place in 1920. González entertained dreams of running for the nation's highest office. But first he had to shed his humiliating nickname as the General Who Never Won A Battle.

Emiliano Zapata always led his troops from the front ranks during armed clashes. Over the years, he had many terrifying close calls with death. Undoubtedly, he wondered how many more battles he could survive. While eating dinner with his men on a night in April 1919, he must have pondered his mortality. Talking to his comrades, he mused about those revered figures in history whose lasting contributions to the human race came long after they were dead. He mentioned Benito Juárez, Abraham Lincoln, and Jesus Christ. Probably the men he ate with noticed his uncharacteristic melancholy mood.

It is ironic that Zapata, who believed betrayal to be the one unforgivable sin, was himself the victim of a traitor. In the spring of 1919, Zapata was approached by Colonel Jesús Guajardo, an officer who was aligned with both President Carranza and General González. Guajardo claimed he was dissatisfied with his present army position and wanted to join the Zapatistas. He vowed to bring with him an entire regiment of men and a much-needed supply of rifles and ammunition. Such side switching was common in revolutionary Mexico, and Zapata decided to investigate this offer. To demonstrate his sincerity, Colonel Guajardo ordered the execution of fifty men who had recently deserted the Zapatista cause and joined his regiment.

Secretly, Guajardo worked closely with General González on a plot to lure Zapata onto open grounds and shoot him. It seemed to be a good plot, and the General Who Never Won A Battle sensed victory at last. He threatened to put Colonel Guajardo in front of a firing squad if any mishaps befouled their plans. Fellow officers said a perfectly terrified Guajardo broke into tears when the general issued this threat.

On April 10, 1919, Emiliano Zapata met with Guajardo at the Chinameca hacienda. This was near Zapata's home grounds. Before the Revolution, he had delivered supplies to this hacienda with his team of mules. Also, Chinameca was the site of one of his earlier battles with the forces of General Huerta. Perhaps the familiarity of the landscape gave Zapata confidence. He talked to Guajardo outside the hacienda gates and the colonel invited him inside for lunch. Zapata rode a magnificent sorrel horse named *As de Oros* (Ace of Diamonds). He had accepted the fine-looking animal as a gift from Guajardo just the previous day.

Zapata took only ten of his soldiers with him as he entered the hacienda. The men saw a company of soldiers standing at attention in the present-arms position. The troops rendered the proper formation to greet a dignitary visiting an army base. A bugler stood on a watchtower, poised to play. One of Zapata's companions, Major Carlos Reyes Avilés, wrote, "Three times the bugle sounded the salute of honor, and as the last note faded away . . . the soldiers who had presented arms fired their rifles twice at point-blank range in the most treacherous, cowardly, and vile manner . . . and our unforgettable General Zapata fell, never to rise again."

Several men in Zapata's party were killed and wounded in the fusillade of bullets. Others escaped by racing out of the hacienda gate. Almost before he tumbled from his horse, soldiers rushed out to grasp Zapata's body. Guajardo instructed his troops to immediately display the body to campesinos as proof that their beloved leader was gone. Zapata was slung over a mule, his arms dangling from one side, his legs the other. Colonel Guajardo took back the marvelous horse, Ace of Diamonds.

The body of Emiliano Zapata surrounded by his comrades

The mule bearing Zapata's remains wound over country roads followed by soldiers. Campesinos drifted out of their huts to join the macabre parade. At one point, the procession came within a half mile of Zapata's birthplace at the village of Anenecuilco. Hundreds more country people joined the assembly as it meandered down the roads.

At the town of Cuautla, an exuberant General González rushed out to greet the party. Finally he had won a battle, as his enemy, the Attila of the South, was dead. Zapata's bullet-ridden corpse was displayed in front of the Cuautla police station, and people were encouraged to pass in front of it as part of a public viewing. Pictures were taken; even a movie camera recorded the event. But whispers rose from the mourners who walked in front of the body: This is not Emiliano Zapata. This is the body of an impostor. Our 'Miliano is alive, somewhere.

The Mexican Revolution ended in 1920, as the violence and bloodshed slowed and finally stopped like a train engine running out of steam. Ten years of warfare had left Mexico a drained land. At least 1 million and perhaps as many as 2 million people had died either directly because of the fighting or through disease and hunger brought about by warfare. The Mexican Revolution of 1910-20 was the bloodiest war ever fought on the North American continent, dwarfing even the United States Civil War of 1861-65.

All the major figures of the Revolution met violent ends. Venustiano Carranza was forced out of the presidency and killed by a warlord in May 1920. Pancho Villa was gunned down on July 20, 1923, as he drove a car through the town of Parral, Chihuahua. According to rumors, Villa was assassinated by angry campesinos whom he had forced off a large ranch that he owned. Alvaro Obregón served one term as president of Mexico. He was assassinated in 1928 as he posed for an artist sketching his picture. The artist was a Catholic fanatic who believed Obregón had treated his church poorly.

Mexico remained an impoverished country in which industrial workers earned little and the vast majority of farmers owned no land. On the surface, it seemed the suffering and death of the Revolution meant nothing at all. Yet the Revolution had profoundly changed the character of the people. Mexicans had suffered a calamity, like an earthquake or a terrible storm, and they had endured it together. They emerged from the calamity as one people. No longer were they Indians, whites, mestizos, farmers, factory workers, northerners, or southerners. Now—for the first time in the nation's history—all were Mexicans. As Octavio Paz wrote, "By means of the Revolution the Mexican people found itself. . . . The Revolution was a sudden immersion of Mexico in her own being. . . ."

And the Revolution brought forth a legend, in Emiliano Zapata. Shunning money and power for himself, Zapata lived and finally died for the campesinos of southern Mexico. As the years passed, his image soared in campesino hearts. Long after his execution, reports claimed that Zapata was seen at twilight storming over the countryside on a magnificent white horse. A legend never dies, and the spirit of Emiliano Zapata inspires the Mexican people even to this day.

Street art depicting Emiliano Zapata

TIMELINE

1879   Born on August 8 in the village of Anenecuilco in the state of Morelos.

1894   Parents, Gabriel Zapata and Cleofas Salazar, die.

1910   Drafted into the army of Mexico; works for stable of Ignacio de la Torres y Mier; returns home from Army; accepts position as village chief; begins distributing lands among peasants.

1911   Leads the Zapatistas to fight a major battle at the town of Yautepec; wins the battle with the help of "dynamite boys;" captures the town of Cuautla in Morelos; meets Francisco Madero in Mexico City; marries Josefa Espejo; issues the Plan of Ayala.

1913   Organizes a separate society in the south.

1914   Occupies Mexico City; meets with Pancho Villa.

1917   Brother, Eufemio, killed by a rival Zapatista officer.

1919   Gunned down by soldiers under the command of Pablo González; body put on display at the town of Cuautla.

SOURCES

CHAPTER ONE: **Making of a Legend**
p. 10,   "I will make them . . ." Enrique Krause, *Mexico: Biography of Power* (New York: HarperCollins, 1997), 304.

CHAPTER TWO: **Troubled Times in Mexico**
p. 16,   "At dawn, when God . . ." Roger Parkinson, *Zapata* (New York: Stein and Day, 1980), 22.
p. 18,   "One of the happiest days . . ." Frank McLynn, *Villa and Zapata* (New York: Carroll & Graf, 2000), 42.
p. 22,   "He could speed away . . ." Krause, *Mexico*, 279.
p. 22,   "especially seductive and charming . . ." Ibid.

CHAPTER THREE: **The Road to Revolution**
p. 35,   "If that bunch from . . ." John Womack Jr., *Zapata and the Mexican Revolution* (New York: Alfred A. Knopf, 1969), 63.
p. 35,   "God brought me into . . ." William Johnson, *Heroic Mexico* (New York: Doubleday, 1968), 157.
p. 36,   "As the rainy season . . ." Parkinson, *Zapata*, 32.

CHAPTER FOUR: **Two Nations on the Brink**
p. 39,   "[The] hacendados of Morelos . . ." Rosa E. King, *Tempest Over Mexico* (Boston: Little, Brown, and Company, 1935), 37.
p. 40,   "Overseers would drive . . ." Ibid., 39.
p. 40,   "lived like beasts because . . ." Ibid., 31.
p. 40,   "There's a fellow over near . . ." Ibid., 59.
pp. 40-41,   "He was in the middle . . ." Krause, *Mexico*, 281-283.
p. 43,   "Thousands thronged to watch . . ." Jonathan Kandell, *La Capital: The Biography of Mexico City* (New York: Random House, 1988), 395.
p. 46,   "Suddenly, [once inside the town] . . ." Parkinson, *Zapata*, 65.
p. 47,   "The first we knew of the Revolution . . ." Krause, *Mexico*, 296-297.
p. 47,   "six of the most terrible days . . ." McLynn, *Villa and Zapata*, 93.
p. 49,   "the wily Zapata and his . . ." King, *Tempest*, 88.
p. 51,   "I was calm until the south rose . . ." Krause, *Mexico*, 285.
p. 51,   "They [the revolutionaries] have loosed . . ." Kandell, *La Capital*, 404.

CHAPTER FIVE: **The Plan of Ayala**
p. 53,   "Quickly close everything . . ." King, *Tempest*, 62-63.
p. 53,   "No Caesar ever rode . . ." Ibid., 63.
p. 53,   "a wild-looking body of men . . ." Ibid., 63.
p. 54,   "Through unfair advantage taken of the law . . ." Womack, *Zapata and the Mexican Revolution*, 79.
p. 55,   "Look, Sr. Madero, if I . . ." Krause, *Mexico*, 286.
p. 56,   "Explain to me what it is . . ." Ibid., 298.
p. 56,   "He sat as through made of iron . . ." King, *Tempest*, 82.

p. 57, "ridiculously pretentious bandits . . ." Womack, *Zapata and the Mexican Revolution*, 123.

p. 58, "He drank heavily and nearly . . ." King, *Tempest*, 83.

p. 58, "Huerta was very, very angry . . ." Ibid., 87.

p. 58, "You can begin counting . . ." Krause, *Mexico*, 287.

pp. 59-61, "[We] declare . . ." "The Plan de Ayala," Illinois State University, http://www.ilstu.edu/class/hist263/docs/ayala.html.

p. 61, "so everyone will know how crazy. . ." Parkinson, *Zapata*, 123.

p. 63, "Now, now, *señora* . . ." King, *Tempest*, 93.

CHAPTER SIX: **Land and Liberty**

p. 65, "If they found you walking . . ." Parkinson, *Zapata*, 130.

p. 67, "Those of the rebels he caught . . ." King, *Tempest*, 94.

p. 68, "The only way we can quiet down . . ." Ibid., 90.

p. 68, "Never shall I forget . . ." Ibid., 90.

p. 68, "I said to myself . . ." Parkinson, *Zapata*, 130.

p. 68, "The savage persecution by the Federals . . ." King, *Tempest*, 94.

p. 69, "All Morelos, as I understand it . . ." Womack, *Zapata and the Mexican Revolution*, 138.

p. 70, "The better we behave . . ." Samuel Brunk, *Emiliano Zapata! Revolution and Betrayal in Mexico* (Albuquerque: University of New Mexico Press, 1995), 73.

p. 70, "Zapata Is the Modern Atilla . . ." Ibid., 46.

p. 71, "He was greatly changed . . ." Parkinson, *Zapata*, 123.

p. 71, "Not until Madero's downfall . . ." Ibid., 139.

p. 75, "That is a responsibility I do not . . ." Kandell, *La Capital*, 418.

p. 76, "I am disposed to accept . . ." Ibid., 420.

CHAPTER SEVEN: **Battling a President**

p. 79, "I can pardon those . . ." Krause, *Mexico*, 287.

p. 79, "It is necessary to clean out . . ." Parkinson, *Zapata*, 153.

p. 80, "with an iron hand and . . ." Womack, *Zapata and the Mexican Revolution*, 162.

p. 80, "Here even the stones are . . ." Krause, *Mexico*, 297.

p. 80, "the state was only a rough . . ." Womack, *Zapata and the Mexican Revolution*, 174.

p. 81, "The government made every effort . . ." King, *Tempest*, 130-131.

p. 83, "left to himself this man is . . ." Brunk, *Emiliano Zapata!*, 99.

p. 83, "Even though I find myself . . ." Ibid., 100.

p. 84, "I bow in respect . . ." King, *Tempest*, 183.

p. 84, "It is impossible not to notice . . ." Octavio Paz, *The Labyrinth of Solitude* (New York: The Grove Press, 1985), 82.

p. 87, "In the port of Veracruz . . ." Parkinson, *Zapata*, 174.

p. 88, "I felt like my blood . . ." Brunk, *Emiliano Zapata! Revolution and Betrayal in Mexico*, 104.

p. 88, "His method of fighting . . ." McLynn, *Villa and Zapata*, 227.

p. 94, "What's the good of this . . ." Parkinson, *Zapata*, 192.

CHAPTER EIGHT: Villa and Zapata

p. 97,   "Young master, would you . . ." Krauss, *Mexico*, 292.

p. 99,   "So many were the bouquets . . ." Parkinson, *Zapata*, 197.

p. 99,   "a decided contrast . . ." Womack, *Zapata and the Mexican Revolution*, 220.

p. 99,   "men who have always slept . . ." Parkinson, *Zapata*, 199.

p. 101,   "How the young ladies showered . . ." Ibid., 200.

p. 101,   "I didn't fight for that . . ." McLynn, *Villa and Zapata*, 277.

p. 101,   "The men who have worked . . ." Ibid., 276.

p. 103,   "The villagers say . . ." Krause, *Mexico*, 298.

pp. 106-107,   "Now that there is money . . ." Ibid., 298.

pp. 108-109,   "What a sight greeted us . . ." King, *Tempest*, 288.

p. 109,   "I asked about Zapata . . ." Ibid., 293-294.

CHAPTER NINE: Fraticide

p. 111,   "What I can't get in my head is . . ." Mariano Azuela, *The Underdogs* (New York: New American Library, 1962), 108.

p. 112,   "Every revolution tries to . . ." Paz, *The Labyrinth of Solitude*, 143-144.

p. 116,   "like a herd of pigs . . ." Womack, *Zapata and the Mexican Revolution*, 268.

p. 117,   "One day I went to . . ." Parkinson, *Zapata*, 218.

p. 117,   "Anyone who directly . . ." Womack, *Zapata and the Mexican Revolution*, 269.

p. 118,   "This is no time to talk . . ." King, *Tempest*, 298-299.

p. 121,   "Citizen Carranza . . ." Womack, *Zapata and the Mexican Revolution*, 319.

p. 121,   "Zapatista trash . . ." Ibid., 322.

CHAPTER TEN: Twilight

p. 124,   "The streets and plazas . . ." Krause, *Mexico*, 300.

p. 127,   "When asking for food . . ." Parkinson, *Zapata*, 226.

p. 127,   "His [Zapata's] normally taciturn . . ." Ibid., 233.

p. 128,   "that the calloused hands . . ." Brunk, *Emiliano Zapata!*, 214.

pp. 130-131,   "Three times the bugle sounded . . ." Krause, *Mexico*, 303.

p. 133,   "By means of the Revolution . . ." Paz, *Labrynth of Solitude*, 148.

BIBLIOGRAPHY

Brunk, Samuel. *Emiliano Zapata! Revolution and Betrayal in Mexico*. Albuquerque: University of New Mexico Press, 1995.

Johnson, William. *Heroic Mexico*. New York: Doubleday, 1968.

Kandell, Jonathan. *La Capital: The Biography of Mexico City*. New York: Random House, 1988.

King, Rosa E. *Tempest Over Mexico*. Boston: Little, Brown, and Company, 1935.

Krause, Enrique. *Mexico: Biography of Power*. New York: HarperCollins, 1997.

McLynn, Frank. *Villa and Zapata*. New York: Carroll & Graf, 2000.

Parkes, Henry Bamford. *A History of Mexico*. Boston: Houghton Mifflin, 1969.

Parkinson, Roger. *Zapata*. New York: Stein and Day, 1980.

Paz, Octavio. *The Labyrinth of Solitude*. New York: The Grove Press, 1985.

Ruíz, Eduardo Ramón. *The Great Rebellion: Mexico 1905-1924*. New York: W. W. Norton & Company, 1982.

Tannenbaum, Frank. *Peace by Revolution: Mexico After 1910*. New York: Columbia University Press, 1966.

Womack, John Jr. *Zapata and the Mexican Revolution*. New York: Alfred A. Knopf, 1969.

WEB SITES

www.indigenouspeople.net/zapata.htm

Multiple stories about Emiliano Zapata.

www.mexconnect.com/.../302-zapata-and-the-intellectuals

An essay on Zapata and Mexico's urban intellectuals.

www.mexonline.com/revolution.htm

A succinct discussion of the Mexican Revolution.

INDEX

PICTURE CREDITS

8:	ClassicStock / Alamy
17:	CuboImages srl / Alamy
19:	Used under license from iStockphoto.com
20-21:	frans lemmens / Alamy
24-25:	Used under license from iStockphoto.com
26:	Vintage Images / Alamy
29:	World History Archive / Alamy
30-31:	D. Hurst / Alamy
34:	The Art Archive / Alamy
38:	Mireille Vautier / Alamy
42-43:	John Mitchell / Alamy
50-51:	Jon Arnold Images Ltd / Alamy
57:	Photos 12 / Alamy
58:	Used under license from iStockphoto.com
60:	Photos 12 / Alamy
64:	Mireille Vautier / Alamy
66-67:	Royal Geographical Society / Alamy
73:	Used under license from iStockphoto.com
76:	Courtesy of Library of Congress
78:	Pictorial Press Ltd / Alamy
86:	United Archives GmbH / Alamy
89:	Courtesy of Library of Congress
90-91:	Courtesy of Gengiskanhg
96 top:	World History Archive / Alamy
102:	Photos 12 / Alamy
104-105:	John Mitchell / Alamy
107:	Photos 12 / Alamy
108:	World Pictures / Alamy
110:	Vintage Images / Alamy
114:	Photos 12 / Alamy
116:	Photos 12 / Alamy
120:	World History Archive / Alamy
122:	The Print Collector / Alamy
125:	Courtesy of Library of Congress
126-127:	INTERFOTO / Alamy
128:	Alicia Clarke / Alamy
131:	Wikipedia
134:	Dorothy Alexander / Alamy